Lauren Burns is an aeronautical engineer, advocate and writer. She has a PhD in aerospace engineering. Since discovering at age twenty-one that she is donor conceived she has worked to elevate personal stories to communicate to the public and policymakers the complex issues that can arise from assisted reproductive treatment for the people created. She has appeared extensively across print, radio and television media including SBS's *Insight*, ABC Radio's *Law Report*, *The Drum* and Fairfax newspapers. In 2014 her story was profiled in a two-part episode of *Australian Story* titled 'Searching for C11', which won the Walkley award for Social Equity Journalism. From 2016 to 2019 Lauren was a board member of the Victorian Assisted Reproductive Treatment Authority (VARTA), which is responsible for the regulation and oversight of Victorian assisted reproductive treatment clinics. She was the first ever donor-conceived person appointed to this position.

Triple Helix

My donor-conceived story

LAUREN BURNS

First published 2022 by University of Queensland Press
PO Box 6042, St Lucia, Queensland 4067 Australia

The University of Queensland Press (UQP) acknowledges the Traditional Owners and their custodianship of the lands on which UQP operates. We pay our respects to their Ancestors and their descendants, who continue cultural and spiritual connections to Country. We recognise their valuable contributions to Australian and global society.

uqp.com.au
reception@uqp.com.au

Speeches from page 196 to 201 are reproduced as recorded in the Hansard for the Victorian Legislative Council on 23 February 2016

Cover design by Christabella Designs
Author photograph by Woodrow Wilson Photography
Typeset in 12/17 pt Bembo Std by Post Pre-press Group, Brisbane
Printed in Australia by McPherson's Printing Group

The University of Queensland Press is assisted by the Australian Government through the Australia Council, its arts funding and advisory body.

A catalogue record for this book is available from the National Library of Australia.

ISBN 978 0 7022 6543 3 (pbk)
ISBN 978 0 7022 6646 1 (epdf)
ISBN 978 0 7022 6647 8 (epub)
ISBN 978 0 7022 6648 5 (kindle)

University of Queensland Press uses papers that are natural, renewable and recyclable products made from wood grown in well-managed forests and other controlled sources. The logging and manufacturing processes conform to the environmental regulations of the country of origin.

For Narelle for her lore, and for Gerry for his love.

The following is true
But the previous was false

Prologue

A disbelieving laugh stuttered from my lips as I stared at my mother sitting beside me on the couch. Her hands shook, her eyes downcast. Shock cast a distant shadow on the horizon.

Moments earlier it was just an ordinary day that promised to be relaxed and uneventful. Workers were enjoying their last sleep-in of the Christmas holidays and those who had partied exceptionally hard still sported the soggy remnants of a New Year's hangover. After coming and going from various travels, I was back in Melbourne living at Mum's house as a university student between the second and third years of my aeronautical engineering degree. Sitting on the lounge-room floor, I strummed my guitar along to a Crowded House tune, enjoying the sunlight streaming in the window. I didn't even notice Mum enter the room and sit down until she called out, 'Lauren. Come over here.'

'Huh?'

'There's something I need to talk to you about.'

Alarm bells rang, although their volume was soft. I put down my guitar and sat beside Mum on the sofa.

'It's not so often these days we're at home together,' Mum began in a wooden tone. 'Now you're over twenty-one and back from overseas, I've decided it's time to tell you something.'

I was precisely twelve days over the age of twenty-one.

'What is it?' I asked. 'You're freaking me out.'

Mum's hands were clenched into fists and her face wore a haunted expression. It must be something bad.

'Are you sick?' I asked.

'No, I'm not sick.'

Relief rose through me. At least it wasn't that.

A pause. 'There's no easy way to say this and I know it will be a shock to you …'

The left corner of her mouth twitched. She said the words, and my mind took flight like a startled bird.

The First Circle

One

I rolled up the legs of my quick-dry trousers and waded carefully into the Green River, flip-flops squelching in the mud. The water was an opaque brown from the spring melt. Gripping the sides of the aluminium canoe I jumped into the front seat, keeping my weight low and centred to avoid tipping. My boyfriend, Gerry, clambered into the back seat. His hazel-green eyes glinted like obsidian as he pushed off the bank with a paddle – launching us on our seven-day, hundred-and-fifty-kilometre journey. I gasped as we left the safety of the eddy and the canoe nose flicked sharply downstream with the swiftly flowing water. The current was strong.

I was thirty-three, my conversation with my mother twelve years behind me.

Earlier that morning we had piled into an outfitter's minivan with a dozen strangers and bumped along rough desert tracks to this put-in point in a forgotten part of Utah. On the way out of Moab I watched pronghorn deer graze beside the deeply corrugated, dusty road until the vibration and warm rays of the sun lulled me into drowsiness. I dozed on and off with my mouth open, head lolling and shaking with the ruts.

After we'd put in, the boats quickly spread out. Soon our only companions were the desert ravens circling overhead and blue-grey herons perched on the river's narrow sandy bottom, staring intently into the water as we paddled past.

'Whoa, Nessie!' I exclaimed as a splashing boil of water erupted from beneath our canoe, spinning the nose off course to the left. 'It feels like there's something lurking down there about to surface,' I murmured, staring into the depths of the opaque murk. Twisting around in my seat, I looked upstream at the sandbar we had just passed. These islands left turbulence in their wake – whirlpools that suctioned water down to the unseen riverbed and spewed it back up again as boils. I sensed a language embedded deep within these sources and sinks that formed and dissolved, like a glimpse into inner depths normally veiled from view.

As Gerry steered from the back I attempted a reverse sweep stroke that overcorrected to the right and we hit a whirlpool that spun our nose upstream. Stroking out of time, Gerry and I bumped paddles. Eventually we got it sorted and, once again facing downstream, I recalled the life we had recently shed like an old skin.

Back in Australia, I had been dogged by a restless sensation. Whole weeks evaporated into all-consuming busyness. Gerry and I shared a long-held dream to throw in the towel on our jobs and break away for a year, road tripping around the United States. It had been idly amusing to dream of escape, but faced with the reality it seemed unachievable. Could we really?

Even after I made arrangements to leave my job the US felt like a mirage that would vanish at any moment. Still, I went through the motions of deconstructing my life. The accumulation of six years living with Gerry in a share house in Melbourne was reduced to a mere car boot full of boxes that I stashed under my mother's house.

Upon arriving in the US, I felt unbalanced by the strange sensation of moving between two worlds; my recent past filled by career, and the unfamiliar country of my present nomadic existence. But after purchasing a 1991 Toyota Seabreeze custom-painted RV camper (nicknamed the Tan Can) and adjusting to the switch in seasons, life assumed a new rhythm. Meandering slowly across California, we skirted Nevada to reach the canyonlands of Utah where we had arranged this river trip.

Sluicing through the muddy waters, our canoe was like a time machine. As we travelled further down the Green River the canyon walls capped by vermilion Navajo sandstone slowly deepened. Older layers of rock gradually revealed themselves like slow-turned pages of an enormous book. The grand cliffs flanking the river were ancient libraries – a repository of what all else has forgotten – with millions of years eloquently distilled down into mere centimetres of strata. In turn, my perceptions began to adjust, resetting to the vastness of the landscape, the tempo of paddling, and the unbounded quality of river time.

As the current cast us around the next bend, golden ripples of concentrated sunlight reflected from the flowing water onto the underside of an overhanging grotto. I stared as the shifting wave patterns cast a million shimmering ripples of cause and effect, oscillating between order and chaos like a radio being tuned. A seep in the grotto supported a hanging garden. The aroma of ferns and orchids filtered down, intermingling with the scent of mud that rose from the suspension of sediments in the river, evoking a childhood memory of another river far away.

In my mind's eye I saw my nine-year-old self transfixed by waves of light dancing across the smooth white bark of an old river red gum. My messy blond hair was pulled back into a ponytail and I peered out from beneath a khaki hat several sizes too big. I watched Dad crouch on the grassy bank. Behind wire-rimmed glasses his blue eyes focused as he dug for worms. After collecting enough he showed me how to bait the hook and we set up our rods on a river bend.

I sat patiently, waiting for something to happen. The rod shivered and I began winding in the line. Dad grabbed the net and helped me land a fish with pale, red-streaked fins. A palette of colours shimmered from its silvery scales as Dad dispatched the flapping rainbow trout with a blunt blow to the head. I wasn't distressed by the death of the fish like I would be now. It simply lay still, eyes vacant, the hook through its lower lip and the line protruding from its open mouth.

'Good on you, son!' said Dad approvingly. 'What a good size!' He often called me 'son'. I broke into a gap-toothed grin, feeling a deep sense of pride at his approval.

Later in the day smoke curled up from a small fire Dad built on the banks of the Goulburn River. He wrapped my fish and a wedge of lemon in aluminium foil and placed it in the coals. We sat together beside the fire, watching the late-afternoon glow fade and the stars of the Milky Way slowly emerge, one by one.

I know now that all we can see of our spiral galaxy is one arm. The rest is hidden by the angle of our own perspective.

Twelve years before launching on the journey down the Green River, Mum said those words that echoed deep within my mind.

'Dad's not your biological father.'

I couldn't compute what she'd said. There was a long pause.

'No. You don't mean it,' I said at last.

'It's true.'

Her words tore a hole in the surprisingly convincing façade of my life. As Mum continued speaking, the idea of the stranger who was my unknown biological father passed through this rent in the fabric of reality to join me in the suburban lounge room. He was a shadowy figure backlit by the sun, blurry and indistinguishable.

I sat in silence. Mum filled the void with words that formed an explanation, as best she could. Artificial insemination by donor. Anonymous. She explained that at the time it was considered shameful and had an unsavoury edge. The emphasis was on protecting the privacy of the donor. The Prince Henry's Hospital she attended had since closed and in all likelihood the records had been destroyed.

'I'm sorry. Your dad and I never told anyone. No-one in the family knows, not a soul. It's a secret. Your dad doesn't know I have told you and I'm not going to tell him.'

My parents had separated when I was two. They had no contact with each other.

Mum knew nothing about the donor. Not even physical characteristics, age or profession. Nothing. She explained that in those days you did not get to choose your donor; you were matched by the doctor. Most donations came from medical students. Judging from my looks the donor was probably tall and fair with blue eyes.

I took in her words but scarcely comprehended their meaning. The conversation was brief and soon petered out into an awkward silence.

With so much left unsaid we both got up and left the room, each feeling stunned for our own reasons. I was at a loss to know how to process this unexpected news. I walked in a daze down the hallway, feeling like there was a layer of foggy glass between me and the world. I stopped in front of a mirror, intrigued by the reflection. There was something different in the familiarity of my own face. Tracing the reflected features with my fingers, it occurred to me I'd always assumed I had my father's nose. Searching the mirror for clues to the puzzle, I noticed the small dot of brown pigment in the otherwise blue iris of my right eye.

When I was a child Mum used to tell me a bedtime story. 'Babies start out as plaster casts on a sort of production line. It's the fairies' job to bring them to life by painting in colours for their eyes, hair and skin. The fairy in charge of eyes had just switched from the brown- to the blue-eyed babies and forgot to clean her brush. That's how you got the brown dot; from a little leftover paint on her paintbrush.'

At the time it seemed a neat and plausible explanation. As an adult I learnt the scientific description – sectoral heterochromia. Cultural myths about people with different-coloured eyes suggest they have the gift of being able to see into two worlds simultaneously: both heaven and hell.

I walked further down the hallway and found myself in Mum's bedroom. I sat on the bed and cradled the telephone to my ear as my fingers instinctively punched the buttons. There was a moment of silence and then it started to ring. Ironically, the person closest to me that day was twenty thousand kilometres away.

I'd met Woodrow, my South African boyfriend, two years earlier after itchy feet and a love of skiing led me on my first solo trip overseas, working at a small mountain resort in Massachusetts.

Woodrow was tall, dark and impossibly handsome. At first I'd found it difficult to believe that he was interested in me. As the snow began to melt on the ski season we felt compelled to find a way to stay together. We visited the British consulate in New York to apply for working visas for the one country that would permit us both entry – the UK. After living and working out the rest of the year in various English bars and restaurants we'd travelled to Woodrow's home in South Africa to stay with his family for two months. I'd had to return to Melbourne to restart my deferred university studies and we were now in the process of trying to obtain a visa for him to settle in Australia.

'Hey babe, how are you?' Woodrow answered the phone. His gentle accent sounded husky.

'I'm sorry, did I wake you?'

'No. I mean, sort of. I'm just waking up.' He yawned. 'I miss you.'

'Yeah, me too.'

A dilemma. Should I allow time for the conversation to settle or tell him straight away?

'Actually, there's something I need to tell you. Something major.'

There was that introduction again, the inept warning of what was to come.

'What is it? You know you can tell me anything.'

'Mum sat me down today, and, well … she told me that Dad … you see … he's not my real father.'

There was a brief silence. I knew what Woodrow was thinking. The words sounded ridiculous, even to me, like I was talking about somebody else.

'What?'

'Yeah, I mean, not my biological father. She used a donor.

Mum doesn't really have much information.' Just like that, medical information and heritage all slipped from my grasp. I forged on. 'She was pretty shaken after she told me. She said Dad doesn't know I know. I'm not going to tell him. I think it would upset him.'

'I'm so sorry. I want to be there, so I can hold you and comfort you.'

'Yeah, I know.' I paused. Questions lingered. Might this guy, the stranger who was my biological father, have other children?

'There's also the possibility there might be half-siblings I don't know about.'

It was one of the most bizarre concepts of the whole situation. They could live in my neighbourhood or be a friend of a friend that I'd met at a party. Maybe, God forbid, I'd dated one. Thank goodness Woodrow was from South Africa. Maybe on some dim level of my subconscious there was an awareness that explained why I felt attracted to men from faraway places. If I met someone from Australia should I ask them to do a DNA test to make sure we weren't related?

'It's all completely mind-blowing. But you know, in some ways you are lucky,' said Woodrow, from far away down the phone line. 'Your dad is still your dad.'

I was silent. Maybe they were wise words, but the news was still raw and I didn't much feel like being told I was lucky.

'Look at it this way: at least you've had someone who's been there to take an interest in your life. Sometimes there's no point looking back into the past. What's done is done. You can't change it.'

A spark flared inside me. *Easy for you to say*, I thought. Woodrow's relationship with his dad had not been easy when he was growing up, but at least he knew who his father was. Maybe he didn't realise he was the one who was lucky.

I ended the conversation and hung up feeling deflated. Instead of acknowledging the trauma of being lied to my entire life, I'd been offered platitudes. Why did he tell me it didn't matter? And what did he mean about not looking back into the past?

I was in a spin for the rest of that day and could think of little else. That night a welter of thoughts whirred through my mind. Usually when I needed to process something I reached for my pen, but I couldn't bring myself to write in my journal. For several days afterwards I suffered terrible insomnia. When I finally got to sleep I dreamt my teeth were falling out.

Two

Not long after Mum's big reveal and the confusing conversation with Woodrow, his visa was granted and he moved to Melbourne. But a year later we broke up. Did I break up with him or did he break up with me? I'm not really sure. I'd already arranged to move out of our shared house into university college accommodation when one evening, on a suspicion, I read his phone messages. My limbs went numb as I realised he was seeing someone else.

In my new digs my neighbour was a friendly guy from Vancouver called Graeme. One day it came up that he was adopted. I wanted to tell him that I knew how he felt, but my mouth physically couldn't form the words. Still, I gravitated towards him, searching for an analogue to my own experience. I harboured a secret desire for understanding that I hadn't been able to find anywhere, least of all within the depths of my own heart where there was only an icy numbness.

A diary entry from that time records:

> I read stories of people finding out they are donor conceived, with the effect of derailing their lives. On the contrary I carry on exactly as before. I know I haven't faced it or accepted it, but I also know the chances of ever finding my genetic father are slim to remote (to impossible). It could be somebody I pass on the street. It is likely I have half-siblings, somewhere. Once again, I shall probably never know.

One afternoon a group of us from college went out to Tropfest, a short-film festival held in the Botanic Gardens of Melbourne. As we searched for a place to sit on the lawns I ran into Woodrow and the girl from the text messages, Soo-Lin. With uncharacteristic sass I turned to Graeme, who I had only just met, with an unusual request.

'Do you mind if we hold hands and pretend we're dating?'

'Sure.'

Good old Canadians.

With my head held high I sauntered past Woodrow and Soo-Lin, holding hands with Graeme.

My phone rang.

'Who was that?' demanded Woodrow. 'What's going on?'

'Oh, you know, I'm living in college now. Things happen quickly. I'm moving on.'

A few weeks later I had dinner at Mum's house and she casually inquired how I was going with 'the news'. Like the stunt I'd pulled with Woodrow I gave the impression that I'd moved on.

'I'm fine. It isn't a big deal,' I replied, quickly shutting the conversation down. But the truth was I wasn't fine. The shock was so great I'd been unable to process 'the news'. It had wounded me in a place I couldn't locate. My brain registered what Mum had told me, but none of it seemed real. Deep inside my emotions remained elusive, hidden from my conscious mind. Some psychological mechanism had frozen them beneath a self-protective carapace of numbness, like an icy waterfall.

Over the past year I'd wanted to tell my friends, but I hadn't known how to bring up the subject. I didn't think they would understand when even I didn't know how to relate to my story. It was private, embarrassing and weird. Stuck in between a shattered old and undefined new reality, daily life felt like watching a movie projected on a screen. I couldn't shake the feeling that this was something I had read in the newspaper about another person. It wasn't me. It wasn't happening to me. Creeping thoughts whispered that I might be delusional, even crazy. Was there any way to tell?

Maybe it was better to just put the whole shameful mess out of my mind and move on. Perhaps Woodrow had been right. What point was there in brooding? The answers simply weren't there. And yet … surely I couldn't have been woken up only to fall back asleep?

As these thoughts whirred around inside my head, my heart clung to the persistence of childhood memories. Despite my parents' separation, as I was growing up Dad had been there as my dad. We fished together on the Goulburn River. On summer days I would go to his house for a spa. Sometimes we drove to an arcade to play video games; Daytona racing was a favourite. Afterwards we would visit a local bistro to buy ice cream. I always chose bubblegum flavour, licking through the rainbow of colours in my scoop. In winter we went to football matches at the MCG and after the game we would run onto the field and kick the footy. I wore my yellow-and-black scarf and barracked for the Richmond Tigers, just like Dad, and his father before him. It was something that had passed down the generations. When I was nineteen, Dad retired interstate and our contact became more sporadic. We shared a love of sports, but held different perspectives on many things, from money to politics to the environment.

Why did it bother me that I had no memories of my biological father when other people kept telling me it shouldn't matter? Was there something wrong with me? Or did the problem lie with the outside world? The unknowable figure of my donor dwelt in the corner of my vision, but however fast I spun around he vanished. Still, I could sense his presence in my periphery, the greatest mystery of my being, like a splinter in my brain.

'Who are you?' I asked this stranger.

'Who are *you*?' replied the unseeable figure.

Who was I?

On the morning of the fourth day on the Green River Gerry and I lay in the tent in each other's arms, luxuriating in the warmth at the boundary where our skin met. This heat, which had soaked into the sleeping bag and our bones, was too intoxicating to dissipate and we abandoned plans for getting up early. Instead I massaged the tight muscles of Gerry's lower back and felt the warmth right through me. As we napped in each other's arms, I melted into a deep sense of peace and stillness where I couldn't say if I was unconscious of my existence or conscious of my non-existence.

On a winter's evening nine years earlier, I was getting ready to head out with a group of university friends to the Night Cat on Johnston Street. We were in a celebratory mood, having just finished the last exam of the semester. In the midst of exuberant drinking and dancing my friend Rachael texted a friend to invite him to join us. Normally he would have said no because he lived too far away, but as chance would have it that week he was house-sitting nearby.

Gerry walked in and I said hello. For years we had existed on the fringes of each other's lives. We were both studying the same degree, but our classes were out of phase by six months. On occasion we crossed paths in a group assignment or lecture. I knew his name and had seen him at the odd party, but we hadn't spoken much. He was quiet, but at random times would drop a hilarious one-liner.

After more drinking and talking most of our group moved onto the dimly red lit dance floor. Limbs loosened by more than a couple of beers, my body swayed to the funky beat. Slowly, by wordless decree, Gerry and I edged over to the fringe of our herd of friends and started dancing closer. He kissed my neck and I detected a subtle quality to his touch, resonant with gentleness. In the whirlwind of beer, kisses, dancing, talking and laughing I lost all awareness of time.

Eventually we surfaced for a late-night souvlaki.

'Would you like my phone number?' I asked as I was about to get in a taxi with Rachael. He nodded.

Our second date was Vietnamese noodles on Brunswick Street and a movie at Cinema Nova. Gerry chose the movie, which turned out to be a dreary drama about dysfunctional families starring Philip Seymour Hoffman. At one point, I wanted to reach out and hold his hand, but was too shy. A few minutes later he grabbed mine and stroked the contours of each finger.

Gerry was calm and unhurried, and I enjoyed spending time in his easy-going company. Over a period of weeks we went for picnics, laughed together over stupid jokes, and wrote down grand ideas in a little notebook. In bed, immune from the busy world around us, we talked until late. Slowly our lips would touch and limbs entangle, like origami folds. Afterwards we slept naked pressed together in a full body snug of skin against skin. I wrapped the vee formed by my big and second toes around the back of his heel to maximise contact. When we awoke in the morning we surrendered the private imaginings of our dreams to each other before they crumbled and faded away.

Snuggled together with him, like now in this tent beside the Green River, I lost the contours of myself in a sense of peace and stillness. It seemed inconceivable that I could be anywhere else, but without a chance alignment of timing would we still be lying here, together?

As the morning sun arced slowly across the sky the shadows of freestanding rock spires were like natural sundials measuring the procession of the day. But by the time we finally packed up and launched back onto the river the sun was overhead and I looked out upon a shadowless, timeless land.

Consulting our plastic-coated river map, I spied a pink X just downstream from our camp. The X had been marked four days earlier by the outfitter's river guide, Lorenzo, after I shyly approached him to ask for recommendations for side trips along the river.

'There's a great gallery of pictographs high up on this mesa that hardly anybody knows about,' Lorenzo had told me as he marked the spot. 'They were painted by the ancestral Puebloan people who used to inhabit the river.'

'What are the pictures of?' I had asked, curious.

'It's hard to say. Some people call them holy ghosts, or shamans.'

Despite our late start Gerry indulged my whim to explore the paintings. Changing course, we paddled up a shallow meander. The canoe bottomed out on the fine sand beneath a cottonwood, its acid-green leaves sharply contrasting with the red rock. A warm breeze ruffled my hair. Idly, I held up my left hand, my palm dry and wrinkled from the arid air. It had assumed the same colour as the river mud. In the absence of mirrors I was starting to forget what I looked like.

Feeling a burst of spontaneity, I left Gerry on the bank to rest and stretch his back. Carrying nothing except the river map shoved down the back of my quick-dry trousers, I scrambled precariously from the reedy bank up a crumbling sheer red sandstone cliff to the flat mesa top. My climb was rewarded by an epic vista of the river twisting like a serpent through kilometres of Badlands – vast resonances of textured, banded colours of ever-deepening sandstone. The landscape thrummed with strange, new possibilities as the canyons branched in fractal patterns, like the structure of some giant brain. The architect of this immense splendour was the humble raindrop and I was struck by the irony that the desert is most shaped by the thing it lacks – water. Much of my life had been shaped by what was missing from it, too.

As I walked along the exposed mesa the sun was a blowtorch tracing an arc that welded the distant mountains to the sky. Cursing my foolishness in not bringing any water, I fantasised about returning to the river to immerse my body in its coolness, as inviting as a lover. But I felt myself driven forward. The sun's rays beat down with a physical pressure that warped my rationality, and the further I journeyed from the river, the faster time and space spun into meaninglessness. My eyes and skull throbbed as reality began to melt beneath the persistence of the blinding, unforgiving light. Yet, instinctively, I sensed a redemptive power in the white-hot sun. As Robyn Davidson notes in her memoir, *Tracks*, the desert is the place to go to shed burdens.

Continuing further around the mesa, I turned up a winding wash and entered a hidden canyon whose cathedral-like cliffs soared skywards, threatening to swallow me whole. I became aware of an unnerving silence that grew in intensity until it filled my mind with a roar. Staring up at the rock slab in front of me I strained my eyes, searching for the paintings. Almost at the top of the canyon wall I spotted an indentation pecked into the darker varnished rock. The mark took the form of a spiral, coiled like a butterfly's tongue. Was the silent roar, as loud as a jet engine at full power, the echo of the people who made the carving? Alone in the cathedral canyon within an immense desert, I stared up at the spiral for a minute, waiting expectantly, but nothing happened. Unsettled, I turned around to begin the journey back.

By now my embarrassingly inadequate flip-flops were full of cactus prickles, the soles shredded by the rough terrain. With my feet cut and bleeding, I found a passable crack to scrabble back down to the level of the river and in the distance heard a faint, 'Cooee.'

'Cooee,' I shouted, and the return call grew louder. Gerry and I walked towards each other and hugged in the middle of the dry riverbed for a long time.

'Where were you?' he asked tightly. 'It's been four hours. I had no idea where you'd gone or even where to begin looking for you.'

Feeling a little scared, like I'd just swerved my car in a near miss, I apologised.

Breaking from our embrace I grabbed Gerry's water bottle and raised it to my cracked lips. But despite drinking deeply and often, I couldn't quench the desert's terrible thirst.

Three

In 1931 Austrian mathematician Kurt Gödel published his famous incompleteness theorems. The work shattered deeply held beliefs that logical systems offered the one true pathway to perfect, absolute truth. Gödel's astonishing proof revealed what others had intuited but nobody before him had been able to prove: that any formal mathematical system – no matter how powerful – is intrinsically incomplete. In other words, the only reality that we can hold on to is that some truths will always lie beyond the boundary of the verifiable. There exist questions that you just can't answer.

A little over a year since Mum's confession, on the surface everything was normal. Our family life continued as before. I was doing well in my studies in aerospace engineering. But below the surface lurked things I kept to myself. Everything had changed. Deep within my own private truth of unprovable feelings I felt like Gödel's daughter; intrinsically incomplete.

Intellectually, I understood what Mum had told me, that Dad and I were genetic strangers. But emotionally, with my childhood behind me, the neural connections identifying my dad as my dad were cemented. Internally, I tried to reconcile the splintered pieces of my identity but there was a problem. In the place where I had inherited half my genes all I could see was a void. By extension I felt part of that void, hollow and empty. I was plagued by a terrible sense of dissonance, fragmentation and desynchronisation, like time itself was standing still. I couldn't make sense of my past, which jumbled my present and clouded my future. My internal narrative, the building block of the self, was confused. I couldn't reconcile the story shaped by my birth certificate and upbringing with the story of the DNA unfurling within my cells. How could I figure out what to believe when what I knew wasn't the same as how I felt? Stuck in the middle of this intolerable paradox, I felt a sensation like I was sliding down my own throat.

'It's true,' Mum had told me, as she confessed that what came before was a lie.

The following is true

But the previous was false

Her words formed a strange, self-referencing loop that was unresolvable. It led me nowhere except into endless branching corridors of questions without answers. It was impossible to discern the truth from the lies when there didn't appear to be a centre, or any way out of this labyrinthine loop. Worst of all, I felt completely alone with nobody to help me figure it out.

Caught in a fog of confusion, I attempted to navigate my situation, not by talking, but by thinking a lot about this person – my donor, or whatever I was supposed to call him. I had so many questions – questions that could not be answered. Where was he? Did our shared genes produce similarities in looks, personality or interests? Did he ever wonder if I existed? Would he want to meet me? If we were to meet, how should I react towards him? Were we family? Hardly. We were strangers and had nothing to do with each other's lives. It was difficult to imagine he was even real, living out there somewhere in the community. Or maybe he had died. It was futile. Trying to find him was like trying to locate silence; he was both everywhere, and nowhere in my life.

Because Dad lived interstate, visits were infrequent. We'd never talked about our feelings, so I decided it was best not to tell him I knew the truth, let alone attempt to explain to him that the questions in my mind about where I came from did not stem from any shortcomings from him. If I had been able to talk to Dad I would have told him my feelings towards him hadn't changed. But the new knowledge that brutally carved up the social and biological aspects of my paternity left me with a peculiar sense of *loss*. I struggled to express my thoughts, the questions I dared not ask or even articulate in my head, because it seemed like a betrayal of loyalty. Better to stay silent. And so I did.

When I looked in the mirror at the unfamiliarity of my own reflection I smiled at this stranger and felt empathy for her, but like Alice through the looking glass she was unreachable. In the mirrored world everything appears identical to the real world, but at a deeper level it is all reversed; left is right and right is left. It wasn't until much later I realised this disassociation was a symptom of shock.

There was only one thing that could penetrate this state or, more accurately, this statelessness of emotion: I was moved by music. In certain songs the combination of rhythm, soaring solos and lyrics was able to connect isolated islands in my brain, allowing me to *feel* something. I would lie in bed listening to music that temporarily returned a sense of substance, power and emotion to reality, and

I would discover dormant emotions: longing, loneliness, desire. An incontinent nostalgia towards something I had never known. It was a release that lasted as long as the music played.

What I realised during those brief flashes of emotional insight was that I wanted to know something about this person who was my donor. I thought this was fair enough, a simple desire to put a human face in place of the void where I inherited half my genes, to know more about my heritage and identity. I wanted to search for him, but had scant information to make this possible. There was no system in place to assist me, and I interpreted this to mean that my desire was a misguided motivation because none of this was supposed to matter to me. I wasn't following the script of how society expected me to react. I was an anomaly. A stray link that had fallen out of the chain.

A couple more times Mum casually tried to inquire how I was going but I brushed her off. Deep down part of me wanted to talk about my confusing feelings, but I couldn't. My lips froze, unable to form the words. My parents had withheld the truth, and my physical body was gripped by the power of this secret. I didn't blame my mother and my anger wasn't directed towards her. I knew that in pursuing artificial insemination she hadn't had a choice in using an anonymous donor. However, if my parents had deliberately chosen an anonymous donor when there were other options available I would have been very angry. I knew Mum was normally a scrupulously honest person, and she was pressured to keep the secret through cultural taboos. I respected her for having the courage to tell me the truth; something that was enormously difficult because by nature she is not confrontational and finds it hard to talk about personal issues. It would have been easier for her to let the years slip by without mentioning anything. Sometimes I felt like she was a victim of telling me the truth, that she needed me to comfort and reassure her that it was all okay. It would be easier for her to hear that I didn't have questions and I didn't need answers.

In short, I needed to get away.

The opportunity for escape presented itself in the form of a six-month engineering internship in Germany offered by my university. Including subsequent travels working another ski season in Canada, I planned to be away from home for exactly one year of wanderlust. And so, eighteen months after the momentous conversation with Mum, aged twenty-two and freshly single, I received a registered parcel in the mail. I tore it open and out dropped a maroon passport embossed with a gold Celtic harp. I opened it to the page which contained my photograph and name. Under nationality was written *Éireannach / Irish.*

I'd inherited my eligibility for Irish citizenship from Mum's father, Robert Hugh Broadberry. Robert had died twenty-five years before I was born and so our personal connection was non-existent. It was only through family memories and the extended research and writing of my aunt Joan that I knew something of the man Mum and Joan called 'Dadda'.

Robert was born in Sallymount Avenue, Dublin, on 27 April 1902. His early life was lived against a backdrop of political turmoil that shaped his later embrace of communism. When he was a teenager he started seeing a girl named Margaret who lived down the street. When Margaret told him she was pregnant they wed, in September 1921, when they were both nineteen years old. There was some suspicion about the timing of the pregnancy and Margaret later admitted to Robert that he was not the baby's father. Even though the marriage did not last, Robert is listed on the birth certificate and the little girl received his surname. She grew up believing that Robert was her biological father who had left before she was born.

Robert had joined the Royal Navy as a stoker when he was seventeen and after this personal scandal he fled to sea for seven years. He left the Royal Navy after working his passage to Port Melbourne on a merchant ship. He lost touch with his family for a long period until about 1950 when he sent a letter to his favourite sister, Norah, informing her he had acquired a wife – my grandmother Grace – and three children. The family resided in a rented terrace house in Carlton, carving out a living letting rooms to about a dozen lodgers. Some of the boarders were transient, others permanent, and all were men.

Robert held strong views about class hierarchy, which centred upon a desire to build a different, better world. He passionately believed that the Soviet Union provided a superior model for how to live and he held an idealistic dream of a society relieved of the suffering caused by unemployment and poverty, in which men and women were equal and education and healthcare were free. Mum almost never brought friends home to play as she dreaded introducing them to her eccentric father who would try to indoctrinate all comers, including children, with pamphlets on Marxist theory.

Mum and her twin sister, Joan, only ever had one birthday party, which their mother, Grace, organised while their father was in hospital. Mum remembered to take down the picture of Jesus Christ that graced the outhouse toilet, but the portrait of Stalin in the living room completely slipped her mind. When her friend Minnie inquired, Mum made up a story that it was actually her uncle who looked quite a lot like Stalin, but doesn't think she was believed.

Although of Irish heritage, Robert was atheist, but he was not without a certain flexibility. Grace was supportive of the children attending church, and in his usual contrary manner Robert did not prevent their enrolment in Sunday School. Thus, Mum's Sunday morning routine began with fire and brimstone preaching at the Church of Christ where the pastor made it clear that non-adherents of the sect were going straight to hell. Church was followed by outings with the Junior Eureka Youth League – a communist-affiliated organisation – in the afternoon.

As a teenager Mum taught Sunday School and won a prize for being able to recite the most verses from the Bible. She also still remembers all the words to 'The Red Flag'. To survive her difficult childhood she learnt to inhabit a strange mental world in which these two parts of her life had to be kept separate and secret. This necessity led her to grow up guarded and lacking in confidence. She had to watch what she said; one wrong word could bring her fragile world crashing down. She reflects now, half jokingly, 'I learnt to compartmentalise.'

From the way Robert dressed in an old shirt, tattered coat and flat working-man's cloth cap, his frequent swearing and political views, Mum and her siblings, Joan and Len, always presumed he was from a working-class background. But he only drank on rare occasions, and didn't smoke, gamble, or follow the local religions of football or cricket.

In 1977, eighteen years after Robert's death, my aunt Joan travelled to the United Kingdom and got in touch with the long-lost Irish Broadberry clan. To her surprise she found her father came from a decidedly upper-middle-class family. Robert had been educated as a boarder at St Vincent's Castleknock College, a prestigious boys' school in Dublin where about a quarter of the boys went on to become ordained priests.

Class background wasn't Robert's only family secret. Joan

discovered a marriage certificate, dated 1935, that lists a woman named Violet May Kayll at the address of the boarding house in Carlton. Violet is also listed as his next of kin on his Royal Australian Navy paperwork. Subsequent searches uncovered two more marriages, to Lily Sharpe in 1939 and Mary Scott in 1940. Adding to his abandoned Irish bride, and my grandmother Grace, that made five marriages. Did Robert get divorced between marriages? Did any of his previous wives die, or have children? We don't know the answers.

For the engineering internship my university assigned me to complete my *Praktikum* in the historic northern German city-state of Bremen, about an hour south-west of Hamburg. I bought a flight to Europe that stopped over in Indonesia for a few days. As I walked the streets of Kuta on the island of Bali my looks were a universal conversation starter.

'Where you from?' asked one Balinese man.

'Australia,' I replied.

'No, no,' he countered. 'You look European. German or Swedish or something.'

A few days later I landed in Frankfurt and began my six-month adventure living and working in Germany. Most people I knew back home thought the German language was not very beautiful, but for some unknown reason I felt drawn to it. I'd already studied several semesters at the Goethe-Institut in Melbourne. In Germany, being immersed in a second language revealed a strange new country of the mind. I was fascinated to learn German words like *Zeitgeist* that conveyed subtle concepts with no direct equivalent in English. I began to realise the unparalleled power of words to direct our ideas and concepts.

The Balinese man was proved right. During my time in Germany I felt an inexplicable sense of belonging and wondered if it was just coincidence that I blended in so seamlessly. The old questions resurfaced: where were my ancestors from? What did they look like? What languages did they speak?

It turned out that even on the other side of the world my thoughts still traversed the same labyrinth.

Shortly after returning to Australia from my internship in Germany, I emerged from the darkness of the underground Melbourne Central train station on my way to class at RMIT University. Squinting into the early morning sunshine, I strode north up the gentle incline of Swanston Street. Just beyond the State Library lawn I paused at an intersection as the traffic light emitted slow beeps. A tram trundled up La Trobe Street with a riddle printed on its flank. *You've heard me before, yet you hear me again, then I die 'til you call me again. What am I?*

The traffic light switched to rapid, high-pitched beeps, signalling the crossing. On the other side of the street I saw a flash and my eyes clamped shut. When I opened them I noticed a stranger walking towards me, strangely illuminated by chaotic beams of light reflecting off the glass and metal of the city street. One of these dazzling rays had caught the face of his watch and reflected into my eyes. Something in his appearance held my attention: salt-and-pepper hair, a long face and a slightly wonky nose. The woollen fabric of his single-breasted suit pulled tight around his waist, but otherwise he looked fit and strong.

I breathed in. Something about his purposeful stride reverberated. The way he stepped up from the balls of his feet was like my own gait. Ten or twelve paces now separated us. As he drew closer I held my breath and my heart began to pound. I couldn't be sure yet.

Four, three, two paces separated us. Our separate glances met and I froze. Mixed into the bright blue ocean of his right eye was a pool of brown pigment. It was an unusual feature. Distinguishing, even.

Might it be him?

Could our paths have crossed simply by chance?

Should I do something?

What?

As these thoughts raced through my mind, I stood passively until my resolve withered away. It was so long ago that I was given away as a gift. Besides, gifts weren't allowed to return themselves to their giver; that would be considered impolite. Still, as I stood rooted to the pavement in confused hesitation I felt drawn to his face. He gave a slight nod of greeting, which I did not return. What could I possibly say? I looked back. But he was gone as abruptly as he had appeared, melting into the city like a handful of snow clasped by a curious child.

Rational thoughts returned. I reasoned the encounter meant nothing; it was just my mind playing tricks on me. As I stood there unsure of what to do another tram passed travelling in the opposite direction and I read the answer to the riddle.

An echo.

While living overseas in Germany I'd missed the Australian landscape and wildlife. Little things like magpie warbles, laughing kookaburras and the raucous screech of cockatoos. I'd always loved the outdoors. During school holidays Mum often took me camping. She would stuff the boot of the car – a brown Holden Gemini – full of bags, eskies, pillows, a hammer, lengths of rope and other knick-knacks until I couldn't see out the rear window. The centrepiece of the camping gear was an old orange-and-brown tent. The design was spacious – you could stand up inside – but difficult for one person to erect on their own. I vividly recall watching Mum huffing and heaving as she struggled to lock the vertical poles into the horizontal roof frame, animating the canvas like a deranged puppeteer. Behind the theatre lay an example of Mum's steely determination. When she put her mind to something she was doggedly stubborn and not afraid to employ unorthodox methods to get it done.

As a keen birdwatcher Mum always kept her binoculars within arm's reach, including when she was driving. On occasion she would suddenly slam on the brakes and lift the binoculars to her eyes. Alarmed, I would turn around, trying to see over the mountain of camping gear to check for traffic.

'Look, a whistling kite,' Mum would exclaim, breathless with excitement.

As I got older I would chide her. 'Mum, you can't just stop suddenly. There could be traffic!'

'Oh, be quiet. I always look,' she would reply, never liking being told what to do.

Just like me.

Four

Since learning the truth from Mum I'd reacted in many ways. First I'd tried not to care, then I'd run away to the other side of the world, and now I decided to try searching for the identity of my sperm donor. This decision really just acknowledged that I'd already been searching for years, scanning faces in public places for a flicker of resemblance, wondering if I would recognise him, or if he would recognise me.

I began my search by retrieving the scraps of information I already knew. While I was living in Germany my mother had applied for non-identifying information about the donor. Since the clinic she had attended at Prince Henry's Hospital in the early 1980s was long defunct she had instead contacted the government-funded Infertility Treatment Authority (ITA), who responded via letter. They referred to my donor father as C11, the donor code the Prince Henry's clinic had used to de-identify him. C11 was the only name I knew him by. The letter from the ITA read:

Dear Barbara,

Please find enclosed a copy of the non-identifying information about your donor which he completed at the time of donation. Please note, that this information is supplied by the donor and therefore is a subjective description. The information on donor C11 is particularly limited as the donor's file is not known to exist. It is impossible to say what happened to this file, although I have uncovered evidence that it may not have been available as far back as 1986. This is an unfortunate but not unheard of situation, given the approach to donor anonymity at the time. However, I want to assure you that records do exist linking a particular person to this donor code. The information indicates that he was born in January 1957.

Below is a listing of all the people from other families born as a result of donor C11. This list has been prepared from information obtained from medical records recently interrogated. Please note that although this information is presumed to be correct, it may be subject to change upon the receipt of further information.

Family Number	Year and Month of Birth	Gender
1	August 1981	Female
2	December 1981	Male
3	July 1984	Male

Please contact either myself or the Manager of Donor Register Services, Helen, if you have any queries about this information or should you wish to discuss this further.

Yours sincerely,

Kate Dobby

Registers Officer

This letter was how I discovered the existence of my three half-siblings: a woman and two men all born to separate families, scattered like dandelion seeds in the wind. I wondered if we shared a resemblance. Perhaps they were as oblivious as I had been. What might they – or all the others who have not yet been told – know of being donor conceived?

The letter from the ITA came with a redacted copy of the original Prince Henry's donor program paperwork. A handwritten form listed the following characteristics for C11:

Height: 5'11"
Hair colour: Fair
Eye colour: Blue
Weight: About 11.5 stone (73 kg)
Race: Caucasian

It wasn't much. These five non-identifying facts writ small in black and white neglected to describe his essence. What did C11 care about? What made him laugh? Did we look alike, or share interests? Did it matter? But it was something, and something was better than nothing.

The next section of the paperwork concerned medical history.

None of my relatives have ever suffered from any inheritable diseases except as follows:

On the dotted line beneath this statement was written *Nil.*

I wouldn't exactly call it a thorough medical history.

Looking more carefully at the file I noticed something had been crossed out. The letters appeared to spell *canc.* Was it the beginning of the word *cancer*? Why had C11 changed his mind and crossed it out?

Also included in the paperwork was the donor statement and consent form.

> Doctor: Kovacs
>
> To: Prince Henry's Hospital, Melbourne
>
> I offer my services as a donor of semen with the understanding that it is your intention to use my semen for purposes of artificial insemination.
>
> I understand that the identity of any recipient shall not be disclosed to me, nor shall you voluntarily reveal my identity to any recipient.

This information was my starting point. It was a sparse trail of breadcrumbs, but it was all I had to follow. My mother cautioned me that success in finding C11 probably wasn't possible. Instead of being deterred I chose to focus on what Dad had taught me – how to win.

I was eight years old when Dad first began taking me down to the local athletics track. He dispensed coaching advice on long jump and told stories of how he competed at school and university in cross-country and sprints. I inferred I had inherited his sporting abilities. He signed me up with the Doncaster Little Athletics Club. Through the eyes of a child I noticed that when I competed well Dad beamed, and when I didn't do well he seemed tense. I trained at the track with Dad regularly after school during the week, and started recording a stream of personal bests.

A couple of months later Dad entered me in the regional finals. To both of our delight I won the long-jump final and qualified for the state championships.

The night before the championships I was incredibly nervous. Butterflies flitted around my stomach all night and I slept fitfully, kept awake by the worry that not getting a good night's sleep could make me compete poorly the next day. I didn't want to let Dad down.

The next morning he picked me up from Mum's house and was uncharacteristically quiet during the drive to the city. He too seemed nervous.

'Just do your best,' were his parting words when he left me in the marshalling room clutching a small bag containing a tape measure and chalk. Some of the other girls seemed to know each other, but after ticking off my name I sat on the ground by myself, stretching and trying to contain my nerves.

The officials led us up the tunnel and we emerged outside at the long-jump runway. My first competition jump was okay. I was relieved my foot found the board and didn't foul. I checked the list and discovered I was in fourth place. The second jump was a little better, but the leader had also improved. As I waited for my third and final jump Dad came down to the fence and called me over.

'You're doing really well; you just need to put everything into this last jump. Make sure your take-off run is *fast*. As you take off, drive *hard* with your left knee to get plenty of height. Remember to extend your legs out in front of you as you land. Good luck. I'll be watching.'

My name was called and I stripped off my tracksuit and lined up on the runway in yellow singlet and green bloomers. This was it. The jangling nerves reached a crescendo that I desperately tried to channel into adrenaline. As I visualised Dad's instructions my focus narrowed into tunnel vision. There was just the runway and landing pit. Everything else was blank. I started my run-up, and began sprinting in rhythm. As the take-off board approached I moved my legs as fast as I could and dipped down a little as I hit the board. Giving the leap everything I had, I sailed high into the air, flying, almost like a bird. I felt free. As my outstretched feet hit the sand I rolled to my left and cleared the sand pit. I stood to the side, watching nervously as one official staked the jump and another read off the measuring tape.

I had won the Under-9 Girls Long Jump State Championship. I looked over the fence and located Dad in the crowd. He was beaming so wide it almost cracked his face. I put on my tracksuit and all the nerves vanished, replaced by euphoric pride. There were some formalities and us three medallists were led to the middle of the field. As my name was called I stood on the winner's dais and received my gold medal from a young sprinter named Catherine Freeman.

After my win Dad placed two hundred dollars in my bank account. His highest reward for achievement was money. Money was important to him because he had grown up without enough of it. I'd been lucky enough to enjoy a middle-class upbringing and money wasn't a strong motivator for me. I competed for the joy and pride I saw on his face, and the sense of satisfaction that came from winning.

Applying the lessons Dad had taught me over my fifteen-year athletics career, together with Mum's characteristic stubborn determination, I searched for ways to find answers from the extremely limited non-identifying information in my possession. Transcending limitations: isn't that what humans do?

Online research uncovered a newspaper article about Victoria's assisted reproductive treatment legislation, which governed the legalities of my situation. I discovered that in the early 1980s the Victorian government commissioned eminent legal mind Dr Louis Waller to chair an inquiry into the new technologies of assisted reproductive treatment. The result of his report was legislation passed in 1984, but not enacted until 1 July 1988, that prohibited the use of anonymous donors. Victorians conceived by gametes donated after July 1988 could apply for information about the identity of their donor parent. Unfortunately, I was born on the wrong side of this cut-off.

Following up the invitation in Mum's letter from the ITA, I sent an email to the manager of donor register services, Helen Kane.

> I am very interested to hear about the present lobbying for equal access for all donor children to the same rights of information, with a precedent from the adoption legislation. I think that given the opportunity I would like to make contact with my donor father. Therefore I'd like to offer my assistance to do whatever I can to help. Mum said you were looking for case studies of experiences from families like us and would like some letters of personal experience. I would be able to write a letter, or any other submissions that you think would be helpful. Please let me know what I can do.

Helen responded the next day.

> Dear Lauren,
>
> It was good to receive your letter.
>
> As I told your mother, the infertility legislation in Victoria has been reviewed by the Victorian Law Reform Commission. The report has been lodged with Rob Hulls who is the Attorney General, and the new deputy premier. Action has been deferred till after the federal election, so there is time for further comment.
>
> Individuals involved in pre-1988 conceptions at present have the right to place a registration on the Voluntary Register. It could

be argued, given the rights of the child are paramount, that all donor-conceived people should have the right to actively seek information, no matter when they were conceived. There are some complexities around what would need to happen if that was so – records are inconsistent depending upon where and when treatment took place, and there would need to be community education in relation to the changed conditions, but there is precedent in adoption law, where all adopted people are able to apply for their original information. Services are provided as part of that, as they could be in this area.

What I talked with your mother about was the power of the individual experience, in that politicians can sometimes hear that, when they can't necessarily hear what organisations are saying. Victoria has a new Minister for Health, and he is responsible for legislation in this area – his name is Daniel Andrews. But the Victorian Law Reform Commission review is with Rob Hulls, as Attorney General. So your comments could be usefully directed to both of them.

Good luck, and please contact me if you need to discuss this.

Helen

Manager, Donor Register Services

Infertility Treatment Authority

I gave Helen a call, and after speaking over the phone we met in person at the ITA office in the city. Helen was short with straight white hair and rimless glasses. She explained to me that the Infertility Treatment Authority was the statutory authority that managed the two Victorian donor registers: the Central Register and the Voluntary Register. The Central Register was the repository of information that allowed people conceived from sperm and eggs donated after 1988 to apply for information about their donor. I was ineligible for the Central Register, but I could try the Voluntary Register, to which donor-conceived people, their parents and donors could add their information in a voluntary capacity to be matched to biological relatives through the donor code.

I joined the Voluntary Register, but there were no matches. It was the first of many dead ends.

My next lead was Prince Henry's Hospital where I was conceived. An internet search turned up old photographs of a boxy, brutalist, grey institution. In 1940 its eleven storeys made it the tallest building in Melbourne, but by 1991 Prince Henry's Hospital was closed. In 1994, under the economic rationalism of the Kennett government, the buildings were demolished so the valuable inner-city site could be sold to the private sector.

I walked along St Kilda Road to the place where the hospital once stood. Nothing remained except for a silver plaque with a black border and an inscription that read in flowing script, *This plaque was commissioned to recognise the Melbourne Homoeopathic Hospital which was relocated to this site in 1885 and renamed Prince Henry's Hospital in September 1934, closing in September 1991*. At the top of the plaque the Australian coat of arms sat alongside the logo of the property developer that must have profited from selling the apartments that now occupied the space.

I learnt from Helen that after Prince Henry's closed in 1991 the patients were redirected to the newly formed Monash Medical Centre at a site in the fast-growing eastern suburbs of Melbourne. The new clinic was an amalgamation of the Prince Henry's and Queen Victoria donor clinics. For some time the old Prince Henry's Hospital donor records were stored in the basement of the new Prince Henry's Institute, co-located on the Monash site, but the institute only conducted scientific research and did not treat patients with fertility issues. Sometime in the late 1990s a decision was made that the donor records were taking up too much space. Fortunately for me (and all the other donor-conceived people conceived there) they weren't destroyed, but once again transferred, this time to the Public Record Office Victoria. There they sat gathering dust for a number of years until they were eventually rediscovered by the Infertility Treatment Authority. This was how the ITA had been able to provide Mum with the non-identifying information about C11 and details of my three half-siblings.

The bottom line of all these historical events was that, unlike someone conceived at the other founding Victorian clinics, there wasn't anybody I could call seeking answers. Prince Henry's simply didn't exist anymore. This gave the search for the truth of my identity a strange quality, like I was trying to summon the memory of a dream. And yet here I stood, a legacy of the defunct clinic, like the silver plaque on St Kilda Road. A person with questions. Despite all my efforts my only leads remained the donor code of C11, a plaque at the site of a demolished hospital, and orphaned records stored somewhere within the Public Record Office that had revealed a few scraps of non-identifying information. I hovered within this disconnected loop between the past and the present, untethered, floating in a fog.

I had a mental image of my donor father, C11, as the moon, and myself as the ocean. We were connected by the invisible force of genetics that, like gravity, transcended our separation. Locked in the embrace of this tidal cycle, I stretched towards the rising moon shining down a million shimmering ripples of cause and effect, to search for clues to my being. But at other times I felt a confusing counterweight of repulsion and wondered if I was wasting time chasing shadows that had nothing to do with me. Or setting myself up for a painful rejection. The whole situation was embarrassing and weird and I didn't like talking about it. Disheartened by my confusion and lack of progress, I would slide back down to low slack tide.

Gerry and I motored along in the Tan Can on a highway that descended in long, strange loops through the deep forests and crystal mountains of southern Colorado. Following the advice of a fellow traveller we'd met in Moab, we were headed towards a place called Chaco Canyon in the remote north-west corner of New Mexico. It was the capital of the ancestral Puebloan people who had made the carvings and paintings along the Green River.

Our past informs our present in ways we are rarely conscious of. The highways in the US Southwest trace pioneer trails; the pioneer trails followed Native American footpaths; the Native American footpaths were established along bighorn sheep tracks; and the bighorn sheep tracks followed faults and breaks in the rock. In this way the road we travelled was an echo connecting us all the way back to the ancient geology of the earth.

As we descended, the forests slowly disappeared and a dry, dusty landscape emerged. Nothing much grew except sagebrush, rice grass, black brush and the occasional spindly, twisted juniper. A handful of faded towns lay within the desert plains, inlaid with a parquetry of urban interstates, fast-food joints and gas stations. On the highway out of one of these towns, just after a Wendy's diner next to a church proclaiming *Jesus Saves,* Gerry steered the Tan Can off the sealed road onto a dirt track.

Rough Road, read the sign.

May Be Impassable.

Travel at Your Own Risk.

Ahead, a lonely, unfathomable road stretched out and disappeared into the vacant horizon. Gerry began weaving the Tan Can left and right at a snail's pace, avoiding the worst of the corrugations. I stared out the window at the empty plains as turkey vultures circled high above in the deep blue sky. Everything appeared washed out, like an overexposed photograph. I gave voice to a gnawing feeling that we were wasting our time.

'Where the hell are we?' I asked Gerry.

'The middle of nowhere, by the looks of things.'

As the kilometres passed, my mood mellowed. Our enforced slowdown had the side effect of revealing the subtle details of the landscape. The desert was mostly still with small movements – the slow swaying of a juniper tree, a puff of white cloud that appeared and evaporated, and the monotonous bobbing of wells extracting oil from unseen depths. My eyelids began to feel heavy. Lulled by vibration and heat, I fell into a place between waking and sleep.

I opened my eyes as we passed a sign in broken masonry welcoming us to the Chaco Culture National Historical Park. Unlike the deep-cut canyonlands of Utah, this was a shallow canyon flanked to the north and south by sandstone cliffs. Wandering into the visitor centre, we saw a sign announcing a ranger-guided tour of a nearby archaeological site called Una Vida. We decided to tag along to get our bearings.

Una Vida lay a short distance from the visitor centre, perched below the north rim of the canyon wall on a small rise overlooking a prominent butte. Our ranger guide wore khaki and sported a close-cropped white beard. His badge listed the intriguing name of G Cornucopia. He led a handful of us around the remains of half-eroded masonry walls standing amid sagebrush, pointing out the different styles of construction. He then stooped and led us through a low, open doorway into a well-preserved building. After waiting for his audience to assemble inside he began his speech.

'I've lived in this area for many years. The folks who visit all ask the same question; they want to know who built Chaco Canyon and for what purpose.'

He paused, letting the question hang in the air.

'There's no doubt the people shaped the space in this canyon for special reasons. But the way we go about answering the mystery of its purpose can tell us something about ourselves.' The ranger grinned. 'That's what I like about Chaco Canyon. It's sort of like a mirror. The meaning we see in this place is often a reflection of our own beliefs.

'Some Native American tribes will tell you that Chaco was the completion of a sacred vision. Others say that Chaco was hell, a place to never go back to or be repeated. The next question people usually ask me is, "Which one was it? Was this place heaven or hell?" I'm telling you both stories are true.'

The ranger walked back outside and we followed like a procession of dutiful ducklings. He stopped and pointed to the butte, a prominent tower of rock several kilometres distant. It rose a hundred and fifty metres in the air, separated from a larger mesa by an eroded plain studded with grasses and low bushes.

'That there is called Fajada Butte. It looks like just another rock tower. But look closely. Do you see on the side of the butte there's a ramp? The Chacoans built that up with earthworks. The ramp connects to a staircase carved into the rock that leads high atop the tower. You can't go up there anymore because it's been damaged from too many visitors, but it's quite the view.

'At the top of the staircase lie three enormous blocks of sandstone in parallel slabs. Behind those slabs a researcher discovered a spiral petroglyph. Now, that wasn't too unusual; spirals are the most common image found in Chaco Canyon. But this particular spiral has special properties. They named it the Sun Dagger. Has anybody heard of it?'

Someone raised their hand. 'Doesn't it keep time?'

G Cornucopia nodded. 'It marks both the solar and lunar cycles. At midday on the summer solstice the rock slabs channel a vertical beam of light that pierces the very centre of the spiral. And the midwinter full moon casts a shadow that traces each spiral arm. But it does more than keep time. The Sun Dagger measures the Metonic cycle – a special event that occurs once every nineteen years when the phases of the sun and the moon come into alignment.'

Cornucopia frowned. 'The real problem was very practical. Corn takes one hundred and twenty days to germinate, flower and fruit and the growing season in this part of the world is one hundred and thirty days long. If the Puebloans didn't find a way to synchronise the solar and lunar calendars with the year, the planting and harvesting of their staple food would gradually fall out of sync. Soon they would miss the narrow window of the growing season, ending in catastrophe.'

I picked up a pinch of dirt between my fingers and sprinkled it into my palm. The grains of sand bore no trace of humus to hold moisture, or other signs of agricultural fertility. Letting the sand fall back to the earth, I raised my hand to ask a question.

'How does Chaco relate to the present day?' I asked Cornucopia.

He grinned. 'The Sun Dagger doesn't just appear on Fajada Butte. It exists in the bighorn sheep's horn, or the arrangement of stars in a galaxy. Even in the packing of DNA. It's only a matter of scale. These stories don't only concern the past; they are happening *everywhen.*'

The Second Circle

Five

Six months after returning to Australia from Germany, the swirl of choice and chance brought Gerry and me together at the Night Cat bar. Not long afterwards I called Helen from the ITA for a chat to see if she had any updates. She passed on the name and number of another woman in a similar situation to me, and suggested it might be helpful if we got in touch. I stared at the name I'd written down on a scrap of paper.

Narelle Grech

I wanted to call her but kept procrastinating. I was nervous about talking to a stranger, and unsure how to introduce myself. Helen spoke to Narelle again and gave me her email address. Writing came more naturally, and I emailed Narelle that same day. She replied, and after emailing a few times back and forth we organised to meet. I joked that I enjoyed long walks on the beach at sunset and she would know me by the red rose in my buttonhole. It did feel a bit like a blind date.

On a fine spring morning I walked into a café and scanned the crowd. I spotted a woman sitting by herself dressed in a bright red coat with long, brown dreadlocks flowing down her back. She looked up and I caught her gaze, searching for a signal. She broke into a cheeky grin.

'Hey! I'm Narelle,' she said, jumping up and throwing her arms wide to give me a warm hug. 'But most people call me Rel.'

'I'm Lauren,' I said into her dreadlocked hair as we embraced. I sat in the empty chair at her table. 'Sorry it took me a while to get in touch. I did want to talk to you. I kept putting it off because it seemed like a heavy topic of conversation to talk to a stranger about.'

'I totally understand. I remember how nervous I was the first time I spoke to anyone about this stuff.'

I smiled. Her manner was kind and understanding. We were similar ages – at twenty-six Rel was two years older than me – and we talked a bit about our studies and hobbies. Rel had done a social work degree and now had a job in child protection, though she was saving up to go to the UK for a year. She loved how passionate I was about aeronautical engineering.

'Is anybody else in your family into flying or aviation?' she asked.

'No.' I smiled wryly. 'Not that I know of.' My decision had always seemed slightly anomalous as both my parents had commerce degrees and were teachers. 'I studied lots of geeky stuff like maths and physics, but my best subject in Year Twelve was actually English. I also studied art.'

'Good on you! I love art.'

The waitress arrived with our coffees and placed them on the table with a clatter. I looked up into Rel's questioning brown eyes.

'So, when did you find out you're donor conceived?'

I took a deep breath and explained that I'd known for over three years, but that I found it difficult to talk about.

'What about you?' I asked, curious to hear another person's story.

She found out when she was fifteen, from her parents. 'Initially I was pretty upset but didn't make that known.' She didn't talk to anyone about it until she was eighteen. 'I was angry that I couldn't find information so I decided to tell the world! I've moved through so many phases like shock, curiosity, anger, loss, grief, disconnection, disempowerment and hopelessness.' Rel punctuated her speech with wide, expressive hand gestures. 'The emotions come in waves. I could talk for hours about the whole journey, but I don't want to overwhelm you.'

As Rel named her feelings I felt as if somebody had lifted a bell jar off me. How come this woman, whom I had only just met, got it, when the people closest to me didn't?

After the waitress served our brunches I told Rel how my initial reaction wasn't anger, it was more like a loss, plus lots of confusion. 'I didn't do anything stereotypically Hollywood like go off the rails, or take heaps of drugs. If anything, my marks at uni improved. In some ways the whole thing just sounded completely ridiculous to me. It felt like a story I'd heard about someone else.'

'I initially laughed and delayed any deeper analysis until a few years later, when I finished high school,' said Rel.

'I laughed too!' I exclaimed.

That wasn't the only similarity. We found we'd both tried to not let it affect us, to move on, but it hadn't worked. Rel said she was much too curious a person to let it go, and just a little stubborn. I could relate to this, too.

'This might sound silly,' I said, smiling, 'but for almost two years it never even occurred to me that my donor is a real-life person, living his life out there somewhere in the community. Like he has a job and stuff.' I sighed, resting my head on my hand. 'I don't know how to explain it. Perhaps I've become a bit more detached.'

'That's actually normal. It's also been documented with adopted people. I think one of the reasons we feel disconnected is because most people don't know other donor-conceived people.'

I sat in thought, processing how Rel had described my reactions as normal.

'You were conceived at Prince Henry's Hospital too, right?' I asked.

'Yep.'

'Maybe we should volunteer at the Public Record Office and then "accidentally" get locked in after closing time so we can roam around and find our records.'

Rel's eyes sparkled. 'I have this dream of us all coming together to form a sort of donor-conceived army. And then we can lay siege on the Public Record Office and get everyone's records out!' And she threw back her head, her laughter ringing out like a bell, her chunky earrings swaying.

I grinned. 'One day the doctors are going to regret using the sperm of smart people like medical students. They might have inadvertently sowed the seeds of their own downfall.'

As our conversation wound on, we realised we had considered many of the same issues.

'Everyone pretends the genetic link isn't important for us,' Rel said, 'but the reason donor conception exists is so at least one parent can be related to their child. It's all so hypocritical. Then they call them the "donor" to deliberately create distance. I prefer to call him my biological father. That makes it seem a bit more concrete to me.'

I agreed. 'Language is important. It frames the way people view the relationships. I feel like I don't have the right words. The only name I have to call my donor, I mean my biological father, is the code C11. How weird is that?'

'T5 is my donor code. I have a blog called *T5's Daughter*.'

'Wow, I like the way you've flipped the script.'

This reminded me of something Helen from the ITA had told me. I explained to Rel that apparently they assigned donor codes at Prince Henry's from the first letter of the donor's surname. My code was C11 because my biological father was the eleventh man with a surname starting with the letter C to join the donor program.

'Whoa! So T5's surname starts with the letter T.'

'That's right.'

'Oh my gosh, this is so exciting. My initials could have been NT!' Rel's eyes welled up. I handed her a napkin which she used to wipe away the tears.

'I carry around a scrap of paper in my wallet with all the non-identifying information on T5. My sister thinks it's sad, but it's all I have. One time Helen told me that T5's surname was of Maltese origin. I was on a tram and I bloody burst into tears! Now I can add this to the list.'

Each detail meant so much when we had so little.

After we'd been talking for a while, I touched her arm. 'It's so good meeting you. These past years I've struggled to find the words and haven't really been that open about it. I've told a couple of people, but that doesn't include some of my best friends. I'm quite a private person and I'm not sure how to bring it up because I don't think people really know what to say. Sometimes their response just makes me feel worse. People like to brag about their family heritage. Clearly it's a thing. Why don't they understand why it might be important for us?'

Rel suggested that some people found it difficult to imagine what it was like for us. 'Even my family, who I love, don't really get it. I keep having to answer all these questions about why I am searching. I'm not looking for a father figure, or money. I've just got all these questions.'

'Me too.' I hesitated. 'Sometimes I feel kind of adrift. I really want to know the answers to questions like, "What nationality is he?" and "What does he look like?" as well as his interests, likes and dislikes. I wish I could trace my talents and flaws.'

'I get that. It's called mirroring. I'm loud and colourful and expressive and really into singing and writing. Nobody else in my family shares those interests so it makes it difficult to nurture them. I think the different attributes a donor-conceived person might have inherited from their donor get suppressed if they don't fit within the family that raises them. It makes me feel like I'm missing something invisible but vital. That sense of knowing where you come from. I feel untethered, like a tree without roots.'

It was a great description. 'And what about half-siblings? How strange to think they might be around Melbourne?'

Rel's eyes widened. 'I know! I hate it when people say I remind them of somebody they know. It really bugs me. What am I supposed to do with that information? When I was studying I made up these posters that read, "Are you my half-brother or half-sister?" with my photo and plastered them over all the uni notice boards. Crazy, huh?'

I'd never thought of doing that.

Rel continued. 'I say I'm curious about my biological father, but there's more to it than that. I miss him. I really do. People want to know how you can miss someone you've never met, or that you might never meet, and I don't know. It's just how I feel. I partly miss him and partly miss myself. I know from work that the most primal need of every child is to be loved, valued and raised by its parents. I honestly feel that not knowing my biological father has brought about in me difficulties that will never be resolved or healed. I find it really hard losing people I've grown close to. It reminds me of that first loss, or rejection, from before I was even born! Strange. I've also really struggled with feelings of abandonment. When I get close to people I get scared. Scared that they'll leave me too. Each loss is a blow to my understanding of myself. The grief keeps getting compounded. The technical term for it is "disenfranchised grief". Unlike normal grief, it gets worse over time, not better. I question my identity on so many levels. That's when I spiral down the rabbit hole.'

I recognised the place she was talking about. It was a tremendous relief to discover I wasn't alone.

When we were winding up, Rel gave me one more piece of advice. 'Don't let others tell you how you should or shouldn't feel, or make you feel bad about searching. The situation you're in is not your fault. And always remember that we are the real experts. Not the doctors or the psychologists or the policymakers.'

It was such a relief to speak to another donor-conceived person. 'Thanks for meeting with me. Talking about it out loud with someone makes it seem much more real.'

'It's good, isn't it?'

'It's like I don't have to explain, or find the right words. You just understand.'

'I'm involved with a group called TangledWebs who advocate for the rights of people born through donor conception. Maybe you'd be interested to meet with them?'

I definitely was.

As I left the café I felt the lightness of leaving the confessional. In meeting another donor-conceived person I discovered an emotional outlet beyond music. For the first time my experience *connected* me to another person, rather than distancing me. Rel understood and validated my feelings of fragmented identity. She furnished me with a new vocabulary, terms like 'mirroring' and 'disenfranchised grief,' and new points of view that I hadn't felt entitled to consider. Most valuably, she gave me the confidence to trust my feelings.

Inspired and energised, I no longer saw myself as an outlier who couldn't conform. Meeting Rel started me on the path of a completely new journey. She gave me permission to begin questioning the ethics of the system of anonymous donation that had created us.

Six

I sat watching Gerry make breakfast. He halved an avocado, each side perfectly flat, scooped the contents onto fresh bread, added slices of tomato and a dash of pepper and toasted it under the grill. We hadn't known each other very long, just a couple of months. The day before, after I'd met Rel, Gerry and I had gone out for a drink and I'd hinted that something had happened, but I'd needed more time to screw up the courage to be more specific.

Butterflies flitted in my stomach as we carried our plates outside to the courtyard. 'I've got something to tell you,' I ventured as we sat in the dappled sunshine beneath a rambling passionfruit vine. 'It's personal,' I added. There it was again, that unhelpful warning.

Despite our many long hours of talking, we had rarely trodden on the turf of the private and sensitive. Gerry rearranged himself awkwardly in his seat, changing the cross of his legs, sitting more upright.

'What is it? You can tell me,' he said, in his usual comfortable and reassuring tone.

My stomach writhed into a knot and my fingers tingled. 'There are only a couple of people who know this about me.'

Pause. My mouth was dry and didn't want to form the words. My heart pounded so hard that I raised my voice a little.

'I don't actually know who my biological father is.'

I felt like my body was turned inside out, but I explained how Mum had told me, and the scant details I had. 'It's really broken my sense of who I am, my identity. I've been—'

Gerry cut in. 'Do you really need to know who this guy is to form your identity? I don't think so. You already have an identity that you can define for yourself.' He spoke in a sympathetic tone that rang hollow inside me.

'But I don't know what makes me the person I am anymore. It's hard to explain. There is so much blank space now; I feel like a stranger to myself.'

'Well, you are this person in front of me: Burnsy, who loves reading books, is smart and has a wonky sense of humour. If you find out who this guy is you will still be all those things.' It seemed he thought this would be reassuring to me, like I was having a bad dream about inhabiting someone else's body and all of a sudden I would realise that I was five foot eight and always had been, and everything would be okay.

'Don't you understand? I don't know who my biological father is.'

'But you had a father who was there for you growing up.'

'Yes, but that's not my point.'

'It's my point. He did contribute to your identity. He took you fishing and cheered for you at the athletics track. This other person hasn't been any part of who you are.'

'Do you think I shouldn't be allowed to know who this other person is?'

'Being allowed is something else. I'm saying you don't need to know who he is to know who you are. It doesn't matter.'

Reeling at his words, my responses became sharp.

'It really does matter. Why can't you see that this is a loss? Maybe you just take your own family for granted. You don't understand how important they are to you.'

'Why would you say that? I love my family.'

'The loss is one thing, but I'm not even allowed to grieve it. I met this woman who is part of a group that calls themselves TangledWebs—'

Gerry laughed before I could continue.

I stared at him coldly. Despite the shining sun I felt goosebumps on my arms. Leaving my half-eaten breakfast on the plate I picked up my bag and marched out the door, channelling all my rage to fight back the hot tears that threatened to spill over.

I drove home in a daze, feeling gutted. If Gerry, who was such a good listener, couldn't understand this part of my life then I didn't think our relationship could go on. The pattern was repeating, just like with Woodrow. It was a shame because I really liked Gerry.

After our fight we were out of contact for several days. During this time I wrote to Helen to follow up on something Rel had mentioned in our meeting.

Hello Helen,

I was wondering if you could answer a question. When I was overseas travelling people constantly mistook me for being northern European (usually Swedish, German or Dutch). I also have an affinity for German (I studied the language and spent six months there last year). I was wondering if you would be able to tell me if you recognise the C11 donor name as being Anglo, German, or indeed any another nationality. Narelle mentioned that you told her you recognised her donor's surname as being Maltese, and I know that was a huge thing for her and meant a great deal.

Thanks

Lauren

On Melbourne Cup Day, the first Tuesday in November, the 'race that stops the nation' was about to start. As the horses lined up in their stalls, the doorbell rang. I opened the front door. There stood Gerry in the carport with scuffs on his white T-shirt, scraped hands and a graze on his elbow.

'What happened?' I asked in surprise.

'I fell off my bike. Here.' He dropped a letter into my hand and left without a word.

I had no idea what to expect, but it quickly became obvious Gerry had been thinking a lot about our conversation, and regretted the way it had played out. *I feel that the way I responded was uncharacteristic*, he wrote. *It was cold and not thought-through. And fucking stupid. I am really sorry and I regret it.* He had realised he'd always viewed donor conception from the point of view of the donors. *Clearly, you can see that I have never considered the implications of this program on the very people it exists to create.*

After reading and re-reading his letter, I called him, relieved.

'Thanks for the note.'

We arranged to meet, and hugged for a long time. This time Gerry listened patiently as we finished our interrupted conversation.

A couple of days later I received a reply from Helen. She said my donor's name was of Anglo-Saxon origin, but that names don't always convey the richness of our ancestry. She concluded by advising that the only way I could get answers to my real questions would be if I had the right to seek information or contact with my donor.

Complicating our relationship, Helen was both an ally and an obstacle to my search. Did she realise how frustrating it was for me, knowing that she was practically sitting on top of the Prince Henry's records and could casually look up the name of my biological father, and give me a tantalising tidbit – that it was an Anglo-sounding name, that it began with the letter C – and nothing more? She knew who C11 was and I didn't. It made me want to scream. I gave her a call to try to get my head around the complicated legal situation and how I might go about changing it.

'What is always so frustrating with a situation like yours, with pre-1988 births from Prince Henry's, is that the information largely exists but no-one is willing to claim the responsibilities that come with the records,' Helen explained.

'How many people might be in my situation?' I replied.

'It's impossible to say how many people were donor conceived prior to 1988, because records weren't kept. Insemination with donor sperm has probably been carried out in private medical practice from the 1940s, but in a clinical setting since about 1974, and later using donor eggs and embryos in IVF treatments. That's all I can tell you. Nobody has the data.'

I tried to stay calm and be reasonable. 'I'm not asking the ITA for any confidential information to be released directly to me. Just for a letter to be sent to my donor ascertaining his wishes. To check if he is open to exchanging information.'

'At the ITA we've done quite a lot of work to gain access to the Prince Henry's records and therefore the timing of your search has been somewhat fortuitous. The real difficulty is there's nothing I can do. If you were conceived after 1988 you would have the right to apply for information on the Central Register and I would follow up without a second thought. Because you were conceived at a time when that legislation doesn't apply, it's a whole different ball game.'

I realised with dismay that I was stuck in a place where bureaucracy feared to tread. I still wanted to scream but kept a lid on it. Helen was a sympathetic gatekeeper. She was on my side. I remembered something she had written to me, *Take heart, and fight just a little bit longer – the battle is not over yet. But it does seem to go on and on.*

I had to channel Mum's steely determination and not give up. Perhaps if I played my cards right, did more reading on the legal situation or looked up the UN Convention on the Rights of the Child, I could frame my arguments in the right way. Or maybe if I was simply charming and nice enough to Helen, one day she would find a way to share with me that Anglo name beginning with the letter C.

After exploring Una Vida it was getting late. We drove out along a road through a break in Chaco Canyon's south wall, searching for a place to spend the night. The deep ruts and corrugations made such slow going that we decided to simply pull off to the side and camp.

Gerry and I sat outside in the mercifully cooling air, drinking a beer. The fine granules of sand under our colourful Peruvian blanket pleasantly radiated the warmth stored from the day. As shadows lengthened into day's end, the golden late afternoon light fell across the dusty landscape. Transfixed, I watched the red sandstone cliffs and then the entire western sky slowly catch ablaze. The rays flared up and the colours peaked, spreading a molten palette of fluorescent orange and gold. As the sun disappeared behind the canyon walls the hallucinatory intensity faded, leaving a remnant orange glow like the small flame that flickers from a fire that is almost extinguished.

We sat for a while longer, watching the sky turn the pale lilac of the desert five-spot flower, whose bloom resembles a cup containing five scarlet drops of wine. Surprisingly quickly, the sunset colours washed out to an exhausted pale ash grey, leaving no trace of what had just occurred.

'Hey Burnsy, I think we need to enforce one strict rule on this trip,' said Gerry, breaking our awed silence.

'What's that?'

'Make sure we watch the sunset every day.'

It was a simple thing, even a cliché. But simple isn't the same as easy.

I nodded solemnly, 'Deal,' then suddenly whooped. 'Now that's freedom!'

Leaning back against Gerry's lithe form I drank half my beer, which made me feel lightheaded. We sat watching the sky in silence for some time, as the gentle blue haze of evening crept over the canyon. Any sadness at the disappearance of the sun was tempered when the first stars became visible. As darkness deepened, the Milky Way began to emerge.

I took another sip of beer. 'It's weird. The Southern Cross is nowhere to be seen. And Orion is upside down.' I paused, reconsidering. 'Or maybe the right way up.'

It wasn't just the beer. The unfamiliar night sky was also making me feel lightheaded – untethered from the things I thought I knew.

'Isn't it funny how each civilisation sees patterns of meaning in the stars?' I asked Gerry. 'Like some sort of cultural Rorschach test.'

Gerry was quiet. Blinking lights from passing aircraft and the occasional shooting star crisscrossed the spiral arm of the Milky Way. 'Some people saw things differently,' he replied at last. 'Indigenous people created meaning not from the connection of stars in the Milky Way, but the blank spaces between them. Like Dark Emu.'

The velvet warmth of the desert night was soothing and lent itself to quiet contemplation. I stared up at the inky blackness and thought about the significance I'd found within the blank space of C11's mystery to my own sense of self. Rubbing my eyes, I groped for a question at the edge of my mind that inextricably faded, like sand slipping through my fingers. All I could recall was its echo; something strongly felt that couldn't be reduced to a definite shape.

'It's not emptiness,' I said finally to Gerry, 'the space between the stars. There're clouds of interstellar dust and particles that pop in and out of existence all the time.'

I returned my gaze to the confetti of stars of the Milky Way. Those distant pinpoints shone down their light from another time. *Isn't it strange?* I thought, as my eyelids began to droop, heavy with sleep. *The furthest you can ever see is in the dark.*

Seven

A month after meeting Rel, she invited me along to TangledWebs's AGM.

I say AGM, but it was actually just six of us sitting together in a Melbourne café.

Rel introduced me to the others: Myf, Damian, Romana and Pauline. Everyone had such extraordinarily interesting stories, there was hardly time to hear the basic outline of each and ask some of the questions that had been churning around in my mind over the past three years.

Myf was a petite, blond, donor-conceived woman about my age who worked as a graphic designer and was TangledWebs's webmaster. She was also studying law part-time. Her deep legal and strategic insights were core to TangledWebs's advocacy work. She found out she was donor conceived during a fight between her parents when they were splitting up. A year later she met her biological father, Michael, after he recognised her from a photograph that appeared on the front page of *The Australian* newspaper on the day after the 2001 federal election. The accompanying article was about a historic meeting of donor-conceived people. Michael went on to help lobby for information rights for donor-conceived people born from assisted reproductive treatments.

Damian was from Adelaide, but had flown to Melbourne for the day. He was a few years older than me, had red hair, was a biology researcher and deeply involved in martial arts. Unusually for the times, his parents had told him from a young age that he was conceived from an anonymous donor. He had initially embraced this identity, and even considered becoming a donor himself, until the birth of his first child spun him 180 degrees on the importance of biological links.

Romana was the mother of a donor-conceived son and another son conceived naturally. She explained in her Canadian accent that she had quickly realised the problems inherent with using an anonymous donor and was now a fierce advocate for the rights of donor-conceived people. I was fascinated to hear that she had been able to make contact with her son's biological father through the clinic – the Royal Women's Hospital – where he was conceived. I made a mental note to follow this up with Helen to check if there was any relevance to my own situation.

Pauline had silver hair, kind eyes and a knowing smile that played at the corner of her lips, giving her the faintly amused expression of an enlightened soul. She was an adopted person who had helped spearhead the fight for adoption law reform in Victoria. After a fifteen-year battle the law was changed in 1984 to unseal previously closed adoption records, reversing the promise of anonymity given to birth parents at the time of the adoption. Pauline had done her own detective work and had already met her mother, but sadly her mother never divulged any details about her father, except that he was a US serviceman.

Pauline had been around a long time and had accumulated vital experiential knowledge. She shared with me that Prince Henry's Hospital – where Rel and I were conceived – had three main sources of donors: Monash medical students, Victorian Police Academy cadets, and students from the Victorian College of the Arts. The academy and college were both situated nearby on St Kilda Road.

Through the AGM and informal conversation over coffee and cake, I learnt a bit more about the group. TangledWebs built upon the work done by Leonie Hewitt and Caroline Lorbach, two recipient mothers who founded the Donor Conception Support Group out of Sydney. The name came from a poem called 'Marmion', by Sir Walter Scott: 'O what a tangled web we weave / When first we practise to deceive!' It was a grassroots international organisation that advocated on behalf of people conceived through third-party reproduction (donor conception and surrogacy), with the goal of making sure everyone has access to information about their genealogical parentage. When it started, this mission was viewed by most as a radical ask with zero chance of success. The common reaction was that donors had been promised anonymity and the status quo of secrecy should remain.

TangledWebs's other mission was to broaden the dominant media coverage of assisted reproductive treatment, which focused on the parent's or parents' journey with infertility, 'heroic' medical practitioners, and the happy ending of the birth of a 'miracle baby'. The group gave voice to us 'miracle babies', now adults, whose method of conception represented only the beginning of our lives. TangledWebs created the space to explore how standard practice of third-party reproduction could result in complexities unfamiliar to most people, such as fragmented identity or fear of accidental incest.

At the end of the meeting, Romana announced happily, 'This has been a historic day. I can still hardly believe we had *four* donor-conceived people sitting in the same room together!'

It was a good day. I'd learnt so much and it was freeing to talk to people with similar histories, who simply got it. I was grateful to be able to plug into an existing organisation and benefit from their combined wisdom and experience. My fellow agitators – Rel, Myf, Damian, Romana, Pauline and others – were all seasoned advocates who knew how to address a minister, do a radio interview and answer the number one FAQ – whether it was ever reasonable to go back on the promise of anonymity given to donors. I was just beginning to cut my teeth in advocacy and didn't know my Legislative Assembly from my Legislative Council.

Pauline and her husband, Gordon, owned a gorgeous Victorian home in Parkville that functioned as TangledWebs's de facto headquarters. The dining-room table faced a courtyard that flooded the kitchen and living areas with light. While we were gathered around this table, Pauline shared a piece of history in the form of an extraordinary letter she had sent, together with her friend Meredith, to the directors of the three Melbourne clinics then offering donor conception in 1979: Prince Henry's, Queen Victoria and the Royal Women's Hospital.

> We are writing to you concerning a matter to which we have given a great deal of thought and about which we feel very deeply.
>
> We are concerned about the long-term legal, social and psychological side effects of artificial insemination by donor

sperm ('A.I.D.') as it is currently practised in our community. Our interest in this matter originates from the fact that we are both adult adoptees who were adopted as babies. We consider that it is likely, or at least that it has not adequately been shown to be unlikely, that the mental anguish which each of us has experienced in attempting to obtain information concerning our biological parents, will be similarly felt by many off spring of A.I.D.

That we are not alone in the feelings which we have experienced is well documented. We refer to the work of Dr John Triseliotis (University of Edinburgh, author of *In Search of Origins*, 1973) whose research, primarily in relation to adopted people, confirms the need in some people to learn about their cultural and hereditary background. We wonder how persons conceived by A.I.D. are to accommodate this need if information concerning their biological parent is non-existent or withheld from them.

Dr Triseliotis states that 'adopted adults have a special psychological task to perform, that is to integrate two biological and two adopted parents into their personality and identity'. We believe that people created by A.I.D. will face the task of integrating three parents into their identity.

It is likely that a significant proportion of people created by A.I.D. will learn the manner of their conception whatever precautions are taken to conceal this fact. As time progresses and more people are created by modern science in order to satisfy the needs of adults to become parents, the rights of these created people should be protected by legislation now.

We do not intend to raise the profound legal implications in this matter. However, these were outlined very explicitly at the Adoption Conference held in Melbourne in May 1978, at a workshop forum discussing A.I.D.

In summary we believe: –

1. All adult persons should have the civil right to knowledge of their genealogical origins.
2. It should be mandatory for the names of the genealogical parents of an infant to be named on the Birth Certificate. The genealogical parents should be regarded as those who contributed the ovum and sperm from which the infant evolved.
3. If for any reason the parents rearing the child are not the genealogical parents then an additional Birth Certificate should be issued.
4. Donors of sperm should be counselled with regard to the long-term implications of that act.
5. A permanent file should be kept and up-dated recording all aspects of the donor; particularly his medical history.

We hope that you will consider these matters. We would appreciate any comments which you may care to express.

Yours faithfully,

Pauline and Meredith

Pauline told us that after sending this letter she was contacted by a social worker from the Prince Henry's clinic, who had previously worked in adoption, who invited Pauline and Meredith to speak to the clinic staff. It was only much later that I realised the social worker Pauline was referring to was none other than Helen from the ITA.

For me, discovering this letter was the smoking gun that proved doctors couldn't claim ignorance of what complications might arise for the people born out of their practice of anonymous artificial insemination by donor. The reforms Pauline and Meredith had called for in 1979, over thirty years ago, were identical to what TangledWebs was fighting for now. It was amazing how prescient the two adopted women had been in predicting the situation I found myself in, and I felt a huge sense of gratitude towards all those in the adoption community who had advocated on my behalf, even before I was born. Correspondingly, I felt a responsibility to pay forward this intergenerational debt and advocate on behalf of voiceless generations yet to be born from current and emerging assisted reproductive biotechnologies (such as genetic selection and CRISPR), who cannot influence the decisions that will impact the most intimate fabric of their lives.

It was a timely moment to get politically active. A recent court ruling had found that the law restricting assisted reproductive treatment to married women who were medically infertile constituted discrimination against single and lesbian women. This had prompted a review, resulting in new legislation going in front of Victorian parliament. The issue of donor-conceived people's access to information about their genetic identity was not on the radar of that review or the subsequent bill before the parliament, but TangledWebs was trying to force it onto the agenda.

At the age of twenty-four, I started writing to MPs and arranged my first meeting with a politician – a man who held a senior position within the Victorian parliament. Luckily, I wasn't alone; Myf was there with me. Remembering Helen's advice about the power of personal stories, I self-consciously and with great difficulty shared a little of the shock of discovering three years earlier that I was donor conceived. These were personal things I hadn't even confided to some of my best friends. After listening to me bare my soul the MP dismissed my plea for help in the search for my anonymous sperm-donor father by clapping a hand on my shoulder. 'What you don't know can't hurt you.' He then concluded our meeting with a fumbled attempt at a joke. 'Don't worry, at least you look normal!'

As he left the room my expression froze into the mask of female humiliation: an awkward smile. It felt devastating to have my story trivialised. This man displayed no sympathy to my genetic bewilderment, my family tension, or the intrusion of discrimination such as unknown medical history in my daily life.

Beyond the insensitive phrasing his views were typical. My family looked normal. I had two parents – a mum and a dad – and just happened to be conceived with the help of a sperm donor. Why did the identity of my biological father matter to me?

I wished I knew how to express the complexity of my feelings, and again felt an inner rage at my own powerlessness. Politicians, friends, even family; no-one seemed to truly get it – except for the people in TangledWebs.

After this debacle I dusted myself off and pressed on, meeting with other members of parliament who held different views, or were persuaded by our personal stories that this was an issue that needed to be addressed. TangledWebs started to gain recognition and traction among a bloc of MPs, and the failure of the bill to address our concerns created a wedge issue. With the vote on the Assisted Reproductive Treatment Bill on a knife edge, the government defused the situation by promising that once the bill was passed they would refer consideration of donor-conceived people's access to information to the Law Reform Committee. The Assisted Reproductive Treatment Bill passed the Victorian upper house by a single vote.

A few weeks later, Gerry presented me with a gift for my birthday. I unwrapped a rectangular box and hinged it open. Nestled inside was a silver spork on which Gerry had engraved a single word.

Agitator

He was right. The hallway mirror now reflected the form of an activist, although I had no idea where this characteristic stemmed from. I just knew that meeting the other members of TangledWebs and getting involved with advocacy felt natural and right. Finally, I'd found a constructive outlet to channel all my impotent rage. I threw myself into the work, powered by a seemingly bottomless well of energy.

Despite the formidable barriers to my personal search, I took a long view and brimmed with a paradoxical feeling of confidence. A voice at the back of my mind whispered that all these laws and authorities and institutions were just artifice. Somehow, we were going to tear them down, because the law couldn't stand in the way of truth. I was going to find C11.

Over this time two selves evolved. I was both an engineering PhD student and a donor-conception advocate. Strange, because nobody else in my family had a PhD or had been heavily involved in political advocacy. I appeared in the media under both guises, taking part in an RMIT postgraduate marketing campaign somewhat ironically titled 'I Am the Author of My Own Story' that aired on television and in cinemas. In parallel, I was interviewed and photographed by a number of journalists who used my personal story to illustrate the legal situation for donor-conceived people born in Victoria before 1988. I had two sets of friends who knew me within these specific contexts, and never the twain should meet. There was only one person who understood me as both of these identities; the overlap in the Venn diagram of my two selves was Gerry.

During the TangledWebs AGM I had been fascinated to hear Romana's story about the Royal Women's Hospital acting as an intermediary allowing her son to get in touch with his donor. I got on the phone to Helen from the ITA who confirmed this was indeed their policy. When donor-conceived people from the pre-1988 era of anonymity contacted the Royal Women's clinic (now called Melbourne IVF) requesting information the clinic would check their patient records and attempt to locate the donor to pass on a message requesting information and/or contact. The donor had the right not to respond, or to only give what information they were comfortable to reveal.

I mulled over this for a while and called Helen back with a proposal.

'Since the Prince Henry's clinic no longer exists, and the ITA has access to the records, could the ITA help me by acting as an intermediary between me and my donor, like they do at Melbourne IVF?' I asked.

I thought it was a reasonable request but the answer was no. There was a legal problem that Helen described as 'a grey area'. Although the ITA had attained a certain level of guardianship over the Prince Henry's donor records, it stopped short of full control.

'The legislation isn't explicit that this is something we can do,' Helen explained.

'But what about Melbourne IVF contacting donors? I don't understand why, if they can do it and it's not against the law, the ITA can't help me.'

'The ITA paid for a legal opinion to try to clarify the situation. The legal advice said that since the legislation does not explicitly give permission for the ITA to take full control of the Prince Henry's records, we aren't authorised to contact the donor on your behalf.'

'How come someone conceived at Melbourne IVF can get a message passed on to their donor? It's crazy that people born in the same state, at the same time, just at different clinics, should have such completely different rights.'

'I'm sorry. The people who drafted the legislation never foresaw the eventuality of a clinic shutting down, and didn't specify what should happen to the records.'

'Okay, so the ITA has legal advice saying one thing. Another lawyer might interpret the situation completely differently. After all, it's not the law, it's just an opinion. Can I see the legal opinion?'

'No. Look, I know it's very frustrating. It makes no sense at all. There's nothing I can do. You need to lobby for the law to change.'

Alarmingly, Helen went on to explain that the Prince Henry's records had not been digitised, and existed only in paper form. In some cases critical information was hand annotated in the margins in pencil or pen. The records were decades old and incredibly fragile. What if something happened to them? My fate was tied to these orphaned paper records that had fallen between the cracks of foresight, legislation and bureaucracy.

After months of banging my head against this particular brick wall I changed tack and returned to the trail of breadcrumbs. I thought about Pauline's experiential knowledge that Prince Henry's was the teaching hospital for Monash medical students, and they often donated sperm. This fit with my aptitude for science. I put this hunch with the other scraps I had gleaned from Helen, namely that the donor code referred to the first initial of his surname, which began with the letter 'C', and that he had an Anglo-sounding name. Maybe this was enough to triangulate to a person, or at least a shortlist of names.

Though I was supposed to be working on my PhD I started conducting research of another kind. After some internet sleuthing I found a database of graduates on the Monash University website.

I didn't know what year level C11 might have been in when he donated so I handwrote a list of male medicine graduates spanning the 1980s with Anglo surnames starting with the letter C. When I'd finished, I stared at the names on the list with a strong intuition that one of them was the name of my biological father. I just didn't know which one. I spent hours searching the internet for these men, now middle-aged doctors, trying to find photographs, looking for something in them that I also recognised in myself.

The only other concrete information I had from the non-identifying information was that C11's date of birth was January 1957. I had an idea to crosscheck the names on my Monash medical graduates list with the birth notices in the newspaper archives. Mum helped by spending a day at the microfiche machine in the State Library looking up the birth notices for January 1957, searching for a match with the names of the medical students. There were no conclusive leads. After coming this far, I had reached yet another dead end.

The frustrated energy of my own disempowerment was a powerful charge that made me even more determined to find answers. I turned to a new but fast-growing technology that seemed like a promising way to transcend limited information: consumer-DNA testing. The pattern in the double helix of my cells was something that couldn't be altered by signing a contract or passing a law. Its objective truth was a compelling reason why Mum had revealed the secret, because she feared that one day I would find out anyway through personalised medical treatment. Joining a DNA database might reveal a close relative, maybe even a half-sibling, or the donor himself. I ordered kits from the main providers, spat into a tube, scraped my cheek with a plastic scraper, boxed up the samples and returned them by post to laboratories in the United States.

While I waited for the results I read in the newspaper that a single spiralling molecule of DNA contains as many atoms as there are stars in a typical galaxy. Each of us is our own private universe.

An email alerted me that the results were ready. With some trepidation and excitement I logged in and clicked on the DNA matches. Disappointingly there was nothing significant, just a bunch of distant cousins. Another dead end. It seemed I was destined to remain a tree without roots. (At the time I wasn't aware of more powerful search techniques, such as the magic of mirror trees, which allow people to locate their biological parents even when the donor hasn't tested.)

With scientific curiosity I downloaded my raw DNA results and opened the text file.

rsid	chromosome	position	allele1	allele2
rs369202065	1	569388	G	G
rs199476136	1	569400	T	T
rs190214723	1	693625	T	T
rs3131972	1	752721	A	G
rs12562034	1	768448	G	G

...

On and on ran the list of numbers and letters. It looked like a computer code. What did it mean? Was there an inherent importance to sharing DNA with someone? Could I point to the location of this significance within the string of letters and numbers I had downloaded? Or was the significance as much in my mind as physically within the strands of DNA? Perhaps only interactions at the human level were of consequence. And yet I clung to the belief that creating a child was not a meaningless act.

I wasn't just seeking to unravel the mystery of my DNA, although any information about medical history or hereditary diseases would have been welcome. The questions I had, which remained half formed and inarticulate, couldn't have been answered even if I had sequenced my entire genome. I was searching for something deeper, beyond the facts, beyond the code, that was still missing from my consciousness.

But the reality was I was trapped in a bureaucratic vortex where endless forms needed to be filled in simply to request permission to fill in more forms. I'd tried my best to follow the trail of breadcrumbs, yet despite all my efforts and years of searching I remained in the same place I'd started. One by one, all my leads had petered out and the trail had gone cold. It seemed the best I could do was search my own reflection for the ancestors staring back at me, waiting to be discovered. But they remained silent. There were no answers. My face reflected in the hallway mirror seemed destined to remain in genetic chiaroscuro, half in darkness, like desert sand dunes at sunset.

From where had I inherited this face? Through black-and-white photos in an old album, I knew Mum's mother, Grace Mildred Paull, had a pale, oval face dusted with freckles. Her delicate complexion contrasted with her athletic physique. It is through memories passed down from my mum, my aunt Joan and my uncle Len that I know the rest. Grace was born on 4 May 1909 in South Yarra, the treasured youngest of seven siblings – six girls and a boy. A generational twenty-four-year age gap separated Grace and her eldest sister, Bella, and they shared more of a mother–daughter bond than a sibling relationship. The family was very proud of their Scottish heritage and often spoke about tartans, bagpipes, clans, lowlanders, highlanders and Bonnie Prince Charlie.

In the heady days just after the end of the Second World War my thirty-six-year-old grandmother Grace – freshly on the rebound from breaking up with her fiancé and possibly worried about getting on in years – attended a dance at the glamorous Trocadero ballroom close to Flinders Street Station. At the dance she met my forty-three-year-old grandfather. Communist Robert had a lifelong fascination with the colour red, and perhaps was subconsciously attracted to Grace's auburn hair. In keeping with social conventions, after they found out she was pregnant they were married, on 3 December 1945 in South Melbourne, not far from the port where Robert first disembarked from his merchant navy ship. My aunt Joan was born in July 1946. The story goes that Grace didn't know she was carrying twins. When my mother, Barbara, arrived unexpectedly a few minutes later, there was only one crib and one baby carriage. Grace's unmarried sister Elsie, closest in age, helped out with the babies.

A question of genetics was formulative for Mum's sense of identity, just as it was for me. In her case it was the experience of being an identical twin – a genetic clone. In the 1940s and 1950s the thinking about twins was different from today. It was commonly believed that they should be kept together as much as possible, and to separate them risked doing them lasting psychological damage. Consequently, Mum and Joan sat next to each other at school, shared a bedroom (and at one point even the same bed), were dressed alike, had the same friends, got the same birthday presents and read the same books. Mum describes it as like growing up as half of a whole, stunting her ability to form a separate identity. Many people couldn't distinguish between the two white-blond girls and referred to them both simply as 'Twinny'. Mum and Joan wanted to be known as two separate people, but couldn't untangle the Gordian knot of their shared DNA. They were too alike, which led to friction.

Grace was a working mother who held down a job as an invoice typist at Lloyd's Buttons and Plastics in Pelham Street, Carlton, a few minutes' walk from her house in Drummond Street. Lloyd's was founded by a kind Hungarian immigrant who anglicised his name to John George Lloyd. The motto of the business was 'As modern as tomorrow'. But the 1950s weren't quite that modern, and a married woman with young children who had a job was socially frowned upon. But Grace liked her job, making friends and enjoying the oasis of normality from her unusual husband and domestic life. Her wages were half that of a man, but she guarded her economic independence. The children went to their mother, not their father, for pocket money.

Travel and books were the portals that helped my grandmother transcend the limits of her own life. Grace used some of the money she earnt at Lloyd's to take her children on holidays to the Grampians, Healesville and Ocean Grove. These trips were taken without Robert, who stayed home to run the boarding house. Grace loved reading and would take the children to Melbourne City Library to borrow books. Mum and Joan's favourite stories were the Billabong series and Enid Blyton, which I also enjoyed as a child.

Charting my maternal family history I found several clues to my identity. Grandfather Robert's political values rippled down the generations, as Mum and I are also left-leaning. Through my grandmother Grace I could trace the high value I place on economic independence. But there were still gaps. For instance, I couldn't find a mirror for the agitator that relished political advocacy.

Perhaps the answers lay in the place where I inherited the other half of my genes, but this remained a vacuum. Instead of a real person, all I could picture of my biological father was a vial of semen in cold storage labelled C11. It made me feel clinical and hollow, like the syringe that had inseminated my mother.

Eight

'Why didn't you tell me the truth earlier?' I asked Mum one Sunday as we sat outside a café eating brunch. Four years after her unexpected revelation, I was finally ready to talk to her about some of the things left unsaid that day.

Mum sighed. 'In the eighties things were different. Counselling about the consequences of what we were doing was not part of the process. The focus was on the medical procedures to give us a baby. From everyone – your dad, the clinic, society – the clear message was to go home and pretend the child was ours.' There was a slight edge to her tone. 'The treatment was new, almost experimental.'

It is commonly believed, but not actually true, that donor conception began in the 1970s or 1980s. In fact, it had been practised in Australia for decades, since at least the 1940s, but operated as something of a cottage industry. Things really cranked up in a clinical setting due to the greatly increased demand for children in the 1970s. This traced back to the decrease in children available for adoption as a result of the rise of feminism, access to contraception and abortion, reduced social stigma and government policies to support single parents, all of which gave women greater choices.

Mum continued. 'The topic never came up in the media like it does today. Also, it was just simpler to keep the secret. I put it to the back of my mind with the thought that it was something I would deal with later. There was so much happening with a pregnancy and looking after a young child that for a while I almost forgot you were different.'

Perhaps consciously she almost forgot, but part of her would have always been aware. 'If you decided not to tell me when I was younger then why did you change your mind?'

Mum avoided eye contact, looking up and away at the blue sky. 'As you got older it weighed on me more and more. I believed you deserved to know the truth. There was just an inner voice telling me it was something I had to do. Maybe I was influenced by the number of secrets I had to keep when I was growing up and wanted things to be different for you. And I was afraid you would find out accidentally, after I was gone, when you couldn't ask questions. If I was ever going to do it that was the time.

'Still, there were good reasons to say nothing. I had no information at all about the donor. Also, I dreaded the embarrassment of family and friends finding out. I did worry too that maybe I was being selfish to think about unburdening myself of the weight of the secret and putting it on you. And I was afraid of how you'd react, that you might be so angry you'd reject me. But in the end my strong instinct that this was something I had to do won out. After finding out all I could from the internet and reading other people's stories I screwed up my courage and rang a woman in Sydney from the Donor Conception Support Group. She was encouraging and just speaking to her was a breakthrough. In over twenty years that was the first time I had said the words "donor conception" out loud.'

'Why did you choose donor conception?' I asked.

Mum shrugged. 'I always knew adoption was not for me. Donor conception was different; the baby would be genetically mine and no-one need ever know.'

My cheeks flushed. 'If you saw the genetic link between you and your baby as important, why was the genetic link between me and my biological father considered disposable?'

The corner of her mouth twitched slightly. 'You don't know what it was like to be in my position.'

'Well, you don't know what it's like to be me.' I sensed the cruelty in the words that were forming, but said them anyway. 'I feel like you think everything turned out okay, because your struggles were greater. At least your experience was considered important enough to have a name – infertility. I don't even have that. I don't even have a word!' I could see I'd upset her, and part of me relished it. *Schadenfreude*, as they say in German.

'I don't know how to reply. The only thing I can say is I always wanted a family and donor conception brought me great happiness. Having you is the best thing I've ever done. I can never regret it. It has meant more to me than you will ever know.'

Looking into her eyes, shiny with tears, I couldn't fathom her pain, just as she couldn't fathom mine. The gulf wasn't just about donor conception. There was something else. A deep trauma. Something so terrible that she couldn't talk about it, the silence reverberating down the generations.

Robert died of a heart attack when Mum and Joan were thirteen and their brother, Len, was only ten. Four years later, just after the girls finished their Year Twelve matriculation exams, their mother,

Grace, collapsed in her bedroom and was rushed to the Alfred Hospital. The children discovered to their shock that Grace had bowel cancer. She never regained consciousness and died on New Year's Day 1964 at age fifty-five. Grace missed out on seeing her daughters' exam results by only a couple of weeks. When the letters arrived in the post Mum and Joan learnt they had both received top marks. Joan was awarded dux of the school. After going to great efforts to prioritise her daughters' education despite the hardship when her husband died, Grace would have been thrilled to see the fruits of her labour so spectacularly rewarded.

After their mother's death the family banded together, with the elderly aunties granted guardianship of the suddenly orphaned teenage children. Being females from a working-class background, Mum and Joan had been shunted into the commercial girls stream and pre-conditioned to leave school at the end of form four to get jobs as typists. Career expectations were low. But after doing so well in their final year of high school both Mum and Joan were awarded scholarships, enabling them to become the first in the family to attend university and move into the professional ranks. They both studied commerce at the University of Melbourne. Len got a job in the public service.

Times were changing and Joan's first year as a high school teacher, 1968, was the year Victorian female teachers received pay equal to their male colleagues. Mum became an accountant, working for a number of years in the private sector before becoming a university lecturer. Later in life, while working full-time and raising a family as a single parent, she somehow carved out time to complete a master's degree in education. None of this might have been possible if Grace had died a year earlier, before the twins finished high school. Without the advantages of family connections, using only quiet brainpower and sheer instinct, Mum managed to claw herself out of her circumstances, attend university and have a successful career. I'm proud of all she has achieved.

Not long after our conversation, Mum sat at home watching the news on television.

'Grey skies with occasional showers couldn't dampen the celebratory atmosphere of Government House as twenty-five new Churchill Fellows, distinguished guests, families and friends gathered for the official presentations,' said the newsreader. 'At the conclusion of formalities, guests were able to relax and enjoy the hospitality of Governor and Mrs de Kretser.' A shot of the governor of Victoria, David de Kretser, flashed up on the television screen.

'He was my treating doctor at the Prince Henry's clinic,' said Mum, in a matter-of-fact voice.

'Who? The governor of Victoria?'

'Yes. I normally don't have a good memory for people and faces, but I do remember him.'

I was cautious. 'My non-identifying paperwork lists the doctor as Kovacs,' I said, referring to Professor Gab Kovacs, former president of the Fertility Society of Australia.

'I can't remember exactly. It was a long time ago.'

This was a crucial point I needed to clarify. I wrote to Helen at the ITA to try to confirm the treating doctor listed in the files. A few days later I received a response from the donor registers officer, Kate Dobby.

Dear Lauren,

I have your mother's Prince Henry's medical file in front of me and unfortunately the answer to your question is not clear. The actual pages listing the insemination do not have a doctor listed on them. This is not unusual. Also, there are no real treatment notes about your mother's treatment in 1983 for you. The file itself is not in date order so it's not easy to follow what happened and when.

I'd say that it appears that your parents were initially 'managed' by Dr Lording with the inseminations possibly being conducted by Dr de Kretser or Dr Kovacs as the treating doctor. Unfortunately these are not definitive answers but maybe if you speak with your mother about this it might help to jog her memory.

More ambiguity. It was disturbing that the medical records from a public hospital were so poor that they didn't even record basic details like who the treating doctor was. Maybe it wasn't the governor. Perhaps it hardly mattered if the story that he was my mother's treating doctor was truth or fiction. At last I had the closest thing to accountability, a face to put to this whole faceless situation.

The next day I drove into uni, sat down in the computer lab and typed out a letter, leaving the details deliberately vague.

Professor David de Kretser, AC
Governor of Victoria
Government House

Dear Prof. de Kretser,

I am writing to you because you were the doctor who facilitated the conception of myself, using artificial insemination with donor sperm. My mother, Barbara Burns, recalls you as her treating doctor when she visited Prince Henry's infertility treatment clinic in the 1980s.

Donor conception benefitted many infertile couples, however

I believe it is important that, if you aren't already, you are made aware of the far-reaching consequences of donor-conception treatment from the perspective of donor-conceived children, such as myself. Achieving conception with donor sperm may have been the end of the clinic's treatment process, but it was the beginning of our lives. Even though it took a generation, it was inevitable our voices would emerge. I am asking for your help, and support for issues faced by donor-conceived people.

Infertility treatment clinics such as Prince Henry's Hospital recruited sperm donors promising secrecy and anonymity, reinforced by donor statement and consent forms, in the absence of any relevant legislation. The practice of donor conception is based on the premise that biological and genetic links are irrelevant and disposable. However, I doubt very much that anybody actually believes this is true, especially in light of changes to the law in regard to adoption anonymity as well as research from medical and social scientists reinforcing the importance of the genetic link.

I have no doubt you understand the importance of the genetic link, based on your role as Patron of the Genealogical Society of Victoria, a society who promises to 'discover a world of family history'.

The testimony of myself and many other donor-conceived people indicates the absence of information about half of our genetic identity leads to a sense of loss, discrimination in daily life such as lack of medical history, loss of knowledge of cultural heritage and half-siblings, and psychological distress at the knowledge that information exists, but is denied to me.

I am not looking to lay blame or punishment; I simply want to make you aware. You were given the privilege of the high office of Governor of Victoria partly based on your prestigious medical background (including pioneering work in donor conception). My hope is that you may wish to exert your influence in a way that positively affects the lives of donor-conceived people in this state. Of course there is no legal obligation for you to do anything at all, but I hope that making you aware of these issues may prompt you to do what you can to help.

I would like to know if you have access to copies of Prince Henry's records that may enable you to act as an intermediary to write to my biological (donor) father to initiate exchange of information, and potentially ask for consent to release identifying information. Please let me know if there is anything else you can do for me in regard to this issue.

Yours faithfully,
Lauren Burns

I printed the letter off at a quarter to five and felt a strange urgency that I had to post it that day. I raced to the post office, bought a stamp and dropped the envelope into the red postbox, feeling both hopeful and impatient.

Luckily, I didn't have long to wait. A week after posting the letter I received an email from the governor.

Dear Lauren,

Thank you for your very thoughtful letter and the issues that you have raised in it. I would be pleased to meet with you and discuss the issues with you. I would like to access your mother's medical records so that I am familiar with all the issues that led to the use of donor conception. That access may take a little time as the files will need to be retrieved from storage. As soon as I have that information I will contact you again to set up a mutually acceptable time to meet you.

I understand that you have sent a copy of your letter to a counsellor who is well versed in the issues that you and others are having to manage. I will speak with her as she will have a better understanding of where the files are located. I trust that you will have no objections if I was to ask for her help in this matter

Kind regards,

David de Kretser

Governor of Victoria

I heard back again the following Monday.

Dear Lauren,

Surprisingly, it has been easy to get your parents' file and I have had the opportunity to refresh my memory about the reasons for the use of donor insemination. I am happy to meet with you at a mutually suitable date and I have asked my Personal Assistant to make a time. I am fairly heavily committed up to Easter and have a period of leave and then a visit to Gallipoli for Anzac Day so it is likely that the appointment will not be until early in May. Could you call Mrs Callander on the number below to make that appointment.

I look forward to seeing you then.

David de Kretser

Governor of Victoria

I sat down and called the aptly named Mrs Callander. She explained that the governor was a very busy man and we settled on a meeting date of Tuesday 12 May at his residence at Government

House. I hung up the phone feeling both elated and grateful that someone as important as the Victorian governor had agreed to meet with me, and stressed and disheartened that a stranger held such power over my life. The appointment was still months away so in the meantime I had to figure out what I could say to persuade him to help me.

The day after seeing Una Vida, Gerry and I retraced the rough, corrugated road back to Chaco Canyon to explore what we'd heard was the greatest of the great houses, Pueblo Bonito.

When we arrived, we found an outer wall containing levels of tapered windows, encircling hundreds of rectangular rooms. Sunk into the plaza were a series of subterranean ceremonial spaces known as kivas. Originally covered by a crisscrossed wooden roof, today the roofless kivas were open to the elements and filled with desert grasses.

The ranger (not G Cornucopia) began her commentary to the small number of people gathered for the tour as overhead a ragged pair of black-and-white turkey vultures circled.

'Pueblo Bonito is shaped like a half-moon covering an area of three acres. It was the largest and tallest building in North America until the skyscrapers built in Chicago in the 1880s. The masonry walls were up to five storeys high and one metre thick, enclosing more than seven hundred rooms. The purpose of all those rooms remains unclear, but we don't think they were residential. Many have no doorways or windows and only a few contained hearths essential for heating and cooking. This wasn't a giant apartment block or city. It had another purpose, but exactly what remains a mystery.'

I stared up at the immense semicircular outer wall. The façade was smooth but in places it had crumbled, exposing the inner core. These jagged remnants formed a confusion of brick edges pointing in all directions.

'Like other buildings in Chaco Canyon there are clues within the architecture. The horizontal wall enclosing the base of Pueblo Bonito's plaza runs east–west. On days of solar equinox the sun rises and sets exactly in line with it. An internal wall bisecting the half circle runs north–south, so every day at noon it casts no shadow. Thus, the main features of the building align to the midpoints of both the day and the year.'

We moved as a group to the north-east section of the outer curved wall. Yellow grasshoppers leapt with a clatter to escape our falling feet.

'We also know this was a place of immense wealth. In just one room of Pueblo Bonito over fifty-six thousand pieces of turquoise were discovered, including one necklace made from two thousand turquoise beads. Archaeologists have found stone tools, macaw feathers, shells and copper bells and cacao traded from Mexico. There's some evidence that pottery was carried all the way in from outlying communities then ritually smashed, unused. Interestingly, hardly any food was actually grown in the canyon. Corn cobs discovered in Chaco have been traced to originate from distant settlements.

'I've spent a lot of time pondering what exactly the people who received all this food and wealth gave in return. As far as we know, nothing tangible was exported from Chaco Canyon. Perhaps it was an early version of the knowledge economy, or simply radiated the power and prestige of the capital. There are theories that Chaco was a gift to the gods, an administrative centre, a university, a bank, or something more.'

I raised my hand. 'Why did the people leave Chaco Canyon?'

'We don't know exactly. But we do know that over time the changes to the landscape became irreversible. The land was fully occupied by people and the forests that supported deer and provided pinyon nuts were cut down. Erosion cut a deep arroyo that channelled the rainwater away from the fields. It became impossible to return to how things had been before.

'At the height of Chaco's wealth and power, collapse must have seemed a very far-fetched concept, but a decades-long drought began in about 1130. With resource scarcity came conflict. The south side of Pueblo Bonito's plaza, formerly open, was enclosed. In about 1150 most of the population migrated to other parts of the Southwest.'

That evening Gerry and I returned to our roadside camp site amid the sagebrush. The land baked under the sun, but as day slowly rolled into night the gentle, silver starlight was like a soothing balm. We sat on the couch at the back of the Tan Can debating the purpose of Pueblo Bonito and Chaco Canyon. A fragment of something G Cornucopia had said the previous day popped into my mind: *Corn takes one hundred and twenty days to germinate, flower and fruit and the growing season in this part of the world is one hundred and thirty days long.*

'Hey,' I said, 'maybe the whole construction of Chaco Canyon – the great houses, Fajada Butte and the Sun Dagger – was a datum to bring order and coherence to time. Maybe that was the most priceless thing of all for an agrarian civilisation.'

I paused, triumphant, but Gerry was quiet, as was his habit, carefully considering what I had said. As the seconds ticked by, I slowly deflated. Sometimes I wondered if he did it on purpose; he appeared to know how to use silence to devastating effect.

'Maybe,' he offered at last. 'But I'm not sure it's as simple as some sort of vast cosmological calendar. Remember what old Cornucopia said about the need to be cautious, that Chaco Canyon is a mirror? Perhaps what you see reflects your own beliefs. After all, the most powerful paradigms are the ones that are invisible, when you don't even know there is a frame.'

Something in Gerry's words triggered a signpost in my brain that pointed towards a question I wanted to ask myself, but couldn't quite articulate. Fragments of memories and events floated up, but a coherent narrative escaped me. Maddeningly, every time I tried to grasp at the question it slipped away.

The next morning Gerry drove the Tan Can back along the bumpy, dusty road. We stopped at the visitor centre and I bought a sticker of the Sun Dagger spiral and stuck it on the wall above the foot of our bed where I would see it every morning. The Sun Dagger unified two ways of measuring time, by synchronising the different cadences of the sun and the moon. In some puzzling way I suspected this spiral, the circle that never quite closes, contained answers to the question on the edge of my consciousness.

Nine

I was sitting on a cold concrete toilet within a graffiti-covered public block at a skate park beside the Yarra River. It was the morning of my meeting with the governor. On the way into Government House, racked with nerves, I had to stop to pee.

After relieving myself I tucked my white short-sleeved shirt into dark grey trousers, the cuffs brushing against the top of my fake-leather boots. My blond hair was pinned into a bun. I was dressed for a job interview. If the governor was vetting me, I had to pass the test. At the basin I masked my nerves by applying a little mascara, trying to actualise my mantra. *Fake it 'til you make it.* So long as nobody could tell I was nervous then it didn't matter about the violent churning in my stomach.

For the hundredth time I debated with myself the best tone and strategy to adopt during my precious forty minutes with the governor. This was my one and only chance to ask a person who could actually access the Prince Henry's records to write a letter to my donor on my behalf. I didn't want to blow it. I needed to find a way to convey how important this request was to me, so that he wouldn't dismiss it, and somehow convince him of an ethical obligation to act, because he had helped to create me. But that strategy didn't work out so well for Frankenstein's monster.

Above all else, I knew I had to remain poised, nice and normal, and not betray any flickers of anger or frustration. Stay in control. Be patient. Dance the tiptoe waltz that is the donor-conceived person's acquired gait.

It was time to meet my maker, so to speak. Getting back in my car I drove a short distance and pulled up at the entrance to Government House, sequestered within manicured parklands adjacent to the Royal Botanic Gardens. The bronze spear-tipped gate was flanked by two sandstone pillars topped with light boxes. Between the entry and exit gates was the British royal coat of arms with the regal lion and a unicorn in chains. According to Scottish legend a free unicorn is a very dangerous beast.

I gave my name to a footman in a small sentry building and the spear-tipped gates swung open, allowing me to drive slowly up the sweeping asphalt driveway nestled within the nineteenth-century mansion's gardens. As I parked near a three-tiered fountain, I suddenly became aware that my ten-year-old hatchback had scratched and dented side panels and bird shit on the windscreen. Nevertheless, a butler appeared and opened the car door for me as politely as if I had arrived in a Rolls-Royce.

Government House was built in 1876, funded by the rivers of money that flowed into state coffers during Victoria's gold rush. The design was modelled on Queen Victoria's summer residence on the Isle of Wight. Three lavish, white wings provided appropriate accommodation for the unsullied stratum of society. The state governor's flag with the Union Jack in the top left corner fluttered atop the forty-four-metre Belvedere tower.

The butler chaperoned me through the arched portico entrance, asking me to sit and wait in the parlour. After a few minutes he returned and showed me through to a drawing room. For a moment I was dazzled by the light from a crystal chandelier reflected off the marble fireplace. My vision cleared, and I saw a man, the architect of the system of anonymous donation that had created me.

David Morritz de Kretser, AC. Even the name sounded distinguished. He held many titles. Companion of the Order of Australia. 2001 Victorian Father of the Year. Conquistador of Male Infertility (nicknamed by some in the donor-conceived community as the Grand Inseminator). Sworn in as governor of Victoria in 2006, he looked the part of a professor. Thin steel-rimmed glasses perched a little low on the bridge of his nose in front of not unkind eyes. Slight vertical furrows marked well-defined cheekbones. A receding line of white hair, fluffy like a kookaburra, gave him a sense of fragility, reinforced by the slightly oversized ears and nose of an ageing man. He wore a dark suit jacket with a small diamond-encrusted gold pin on the lapel, a pale-blue shirt, no tie, and grey trousers. Unlike mine, his shoes looked like they were made from real leather.

I introduced myself as Lauren and he introduced himself as David. He had a warm, charismatic smile, but something in his gaze made me feel like I was being observed with a slightly detached, scientific air. We settled into two armchairs in front of the marble fireplace with his golden labrador sprawled on the hearth. I felt nervous and strange, like I had accidentally stumbled through a portal into nineteenth-century Britain. Staff, who in another era might have been called servants, brought us tea and cakes, reinforcing the feeling of being in a time warp. I was an ordinary person who had somehow been admitted into the inner sanctum of the highest echelon of society where the real power lies. I wasn't quite sure how to behave or what etiquette was appropriate. My mind raced over the following points:

He is The Honourable Governor of Victoria. I have no title.

He is a member of the academy. I am a student.

He is part of the medical fraternity. I am a young woman with questions.

He is a decorated world expert in male infertility. What do I know?

For reassurance, I thought back to Rel's advice: *Always remember that we are the real experts*. He was looking at me expectantly.

And then my mind went blank.

Luckily, the governor filled the silence by introducing me to his labrador, explaining that Cosmo was a failed guide dog that he kept on as a pet. After giving Cosmo a pat, I asked the governor how the Prince Henry's clinic came about.

'I've been involved in clinical research into andrology and male infertility for over thirty years. I established the clinic at Prince Henry's Hospital to treat couples with infertility.'

He then launched into a long and detailed explanation of the background and history of the Prince Henry's donor program. As the governor explained the finer details of the donor-conception system he helped develop, he noted that the scientific technique – namely artificial insemination by donor – had been well established in the United States and proven to be safe, so consequently no ethical approval was required to begin operating the Prince Henry's clinic. I was reminded again of Gödel's incompleteness theorem – that within every system there exists elusive truths based on strange, self-referencing loops, which the system is blind to. Perhaps I was a practical example, as the governor didn't seem attuned to the reasons I was there.

'Have you ever met an adult donor-conceived person before?' I asked.

'No, you are the first donor baby I've met.'

The muscle in my right eye spasmed. 'As you see, I'm not a baby. I'm an adult.'

'Of course.'

There was a short silence.

The governor continued. 'When I received your letter, I refreshed my memory as to your parents' medical records. I remembered the reason I chose this particular donor was because your parents were both well educated.'

Outwardly I maintained polite attention, but inwardly I fumed as the governor sat there casually talking about C11, reminding me that he chose him and that he knew who he was. Oh, the indignity. It was just like being on the phone with Helen! Was it right that this one man was the gatekeeper holding the keys to the intimate knowledge of my life in his hands?

As a young woman confronting the powers of government and the medical fraternity, my search had taught me the necessity of oscillating between the hunter and the prey, depending on what I judged most advantageous for the outcome I was seeking. Forced by circumstance to walk a delicate tightrope of charm and cunning, at this moment I smiled and tried to be likeable while on the inside I stalked my quarry, carefully sniffing the air. My precious allotted time with the governor was slipping away fast. I needed to switch the conversation away from a medical focus on infertility, towards the human aspects. Somehow, I needed to convey to the governor the impact of his past practices on my life.

The non-identifying paperwork that I received from the ITA dated C11's sperm donation to 1979 and I wasn't conceived until 1983. For four years half my genes had been frozen in a straw immersed in liquid nitrogen. Similarly, for the past four years I had floated in an emotional numbness. I had been thawed by the doctor once. Now, again, I needed a release from suspended animation. But how could I convey to him what it was really like to live this life, the questions without answers that raced endlessly through my mind?

I felt the familiar nerves, like I was nine years old and competing at the state championships again, standing at the end of the runway with a tunnel focus on my final jump. My task was to channel the adrenaline-induced butterflies fluttering around my stomach into maximum effort and flawless execution. Drawing on all the steely determination and competitiveness that Dad had instilled in me, that had helped me break down barriers and solve puzzles to get this far, the analytical side of my brain quickly weighed up my options and decided the best approach was to appeal to his integrity as a doctor. Even though I wasn't his patient, I could try to invoke in him a duty of care. I began my final sprint.

'My purpose in being here today is to tell you a little about my personal story – what being donor conceived means to me in my everyday life. You helped a grateful couple deliver a healthy baby and that probably seemed like the end of things, but it was only the beginning of my life. Being donor conceived by an anonymous donor affects me in so many ways. When I go to the doctor it's distressing because I can't answer basic questions about my medical history. I don't know if there's something I'm missing, maybe cancer, or heart disease. Surely, as a doctor you understand the importance of being able to answer those questions as truthfully and accurately as possible.'

He nodded.

It was a good sign, and I continued. 'There are also social impacts. I don't know who my half-siblings are. I've been told that there are at least three, and there might be more if the donor has children. We are all similar ages and probably located in the geographic area of Melbourne. I'm worried about making unwitting contact, or maybe even dating one. I know statistically it's unlikely, but it's not just a matter of rationally justifying away the anxiety. When I'm out in public, walking down the street or on a tram, I find myself scanning faces in the crowd, searching for someone I might recognise. One day I was walking through the city to class and I thought I saw my donor on the street. It was probably just a random stranger, but I had no way to know for sure. Sometimes people tell me that I look just like their friend, and it drives me crazy because there is nothing I can do to check if they might be a half-sibling.

'I have so many questions I can't answer. Questions about the past, about where I might have come from, and questions about the future, in case I have children of my own and these medical and social impacts pass down to the next generation.'

He sat with his arms crossed, maintaining eye contact, listening carefully.

'In the place where I inherited half my genes, instead of a person, all I see is a vial of semen in cold storage labelled C11. I don't really know who I am. I feel hollow,' I searched my memory for the way Rel had described this feeling, 'like a tree without roots.'

There were things I didn't tell him that were even more personal. How strange it felt to be created by splicing together genes from two people who were never in love, never danced together, had never even met one another.

His charismatic smile was gone and the governor's face was grave.

'Sperm that was used before 1988 was donated on the understanding that the donor would remain anonymous and their identity would not be released unless they consented. It's a difficult balance; I promised people anonymity and you are asking me to go back on that promise.'

His words reminded me of the 1613 Two Row Wampum treaty, which was enacted between the Iroquois tribe and the Dutch government concerning the land that is now upstate New York. It is a treaty without words, consisting of a woven belt of two parallel rows of purple wampum beads set against a backdrop of white beads. The purple rows symbolise two canoes travelling down the river of life, never touching or overlapping. The essence of the treaty is the Iroquois and Dutch tribes agreed to live parallel lives, free from interference from one another.

Professor de Kretser and his colleagues wove a similar treaty or contract, promising two parallel lives for the parents I grew up with and my biological father. The donor statement and consent form that had been included with my non-identifying information read, *I understand that the identity of any recipient shall not be disclosed to me, nor shall you voluntarily reveal my identity to any recipient.*

The governor had promised never to reveal the donor's identity to the recipient woman, my mother, and vice versa. What was missing in this consent form was any mention of me. Now I sought to retrospectively weave a row of beads that navigated between two parallel worlds. Whether this was even possible I wasn't sure, but I wanted the chance to at least try.

Our time was almost up. This was it. I took a deep breath.

'I respect the right of my donor to remain anonymous if that is what he chooses. I'm just asking for you to ask the question, to send a letter to find out his wishes with respect to exchange of information and contact. Please don't dismiss me. I've been searching for a long time. As the treating doctor you are the only person authorised to access those donor records. It's my understanding that if you decide to, you have the capability to make contact with my donor. Would you be willing to write to him on my behalf?'

I paused. What more could I say?

'Please.'

Did I detect a flicker of irritation cross his face? It must be slightly annoying, having to deal with a renegade miracle baby. Couldn't I just shut up and be grateful? He paused, eyes raised in reflection, and I held my breath. Governor of the State. Governor of My Future. Everything hung on the personal ethics of one man.

'I need to consult with a colleague first, and then I'll consider your request,' he replied quietly.

Our time was up. As I got up to leave, I shook his hand.

'Thank you for agreeing to meet with me. You are a man of high integrity.' I meant what I said.

I left the meeting with the feeling that I hadn't succeeded, and yet I hadn't failed. He didn't say yes, but he didn't say no.

I appreciated the governor's dilemma, but if he agreed to write the letter then my biological father would still have a choice. He could choose not to respond at all. That would be a legitimate choice and I think I could deal with that. On the other hand, I never had a choice.

Patience. Yet again I had to wait for the actions of others to dictate my life. Everything sat balanced on a knife edge. A month passed. My emotions were a tightly wound spring, twisting in tighter and tighter spirals. The spring was formed from three strands: determination, made from the hardest tempered steel; vulnerability, made of fragile human flesh; and hope, fresh and springy like a sapling. As the tension of waiting ratcheted up, the steel strand started to cut into the fragile flesh of my vulnerability. I worried that I couldn't keep it together much longer. At some point I was going to snap

My next contact from the governor was an email raising some concerns about my wish to contact the donor. His email recounted things that he could only have learnt from Helen. After realising this, I called her and ended up exploding with rage fuelled by a deep sense of frustration. My internal narrative was that I had shared with Helen my deepest fears in what I thought was a confidential counselling setting, and she had passed these things on to the governor who might now use them as a reason to deny my request. It felt like a betrayal that could jeopardise everything I'd worked so hard for. After all my careful planning and efforts, everything was turning to shit. I was annoyed at myself, and felt like an idiot for not foreseeing this trap, for allowing myself the luxury of letting my guard down and opening up to Helen about my real fears and emotions, instead of maintaining the discipline of playing the game more strategically.

After I calmed down, another internal voice whispered that Helen was doing her best to walk her own delicate tightrope and discharge her duty of care as a counsellor. I admonished myself. Why had I yelled at Helen, who was trying her best to help me? Normally I had a sunny, laid-back nature. I wasn't someone who was prone to explosions. This wasn't me. I felt ashamed. The Sisyphean task was driving me mad.

Helen wrote that because of our 'personality clash' she

had referred me on to another counsellor at the ITA named Kate Bourne. She also let me know that she had decided to resign from the ITA and would be leaving the next month.

I was sorry it had ended with a rift between us. We had spent hours talking on the phone as Helen patiently answered my endless questions, helping me piece together an understanding of the legal situation and how it related to my case. Helen had injected a sense of humanity into an unfeeling system, and provided useful advice and welcome encouragement. I felt that she connected me to my past, as she had been a social worker at Prince Henry's Hospital in the 1980s. With this insider knowledge, she had been able to tell me the meaning of my donor code C11. It was Helen who had introduced me to Rel, and all that followed.

A month and a half after our meeting I heard from the governor again.

> Dear Lauren,
>
> I am awaiting the return of a colleague who is currently overseas who has already travelled this pathway of contacting a donor. Once I have spoken to him it is likely that I will continue to progress the contact that you seek. I cannot predict the outcome but I am prepared to follow through the process. I will be in touch when I have any further information.
>
> Kind regards,
> David de Kretser
> Governor of Victoria

Almost three months after my meeting with the governor I received another email from him.

Dear Lauren,

I have spoken to my colleague who has traversed this path before and with his advice, I have sent a letter to the donor involved to ascertain whether he is willing to explore the issue further and suggested that he contact me in the first instance. In the meantime, you may want to establish contact with the counsellor. I will be in touch when I have any further information. Please be patient.

Best wishes,

David de Kretser

Governor of Victoria

Despite the obvious excitement of having at last managed to arrange for a message to be sent to my biological father, I didn't have any expectations of receiving a response. In nearly five years of searching, progress always happened at a glacial pace. If C11 was going to reply, I expected I would have to wait a very long time for it.

But a week after the governor's email things suddenly sped up. I got a phone call from my new donor-linking counsellor, Kate Bourne, who asked me to come into the ITA office. During this meeting I was stunned when she told me that C11 had already responded to the governor's letter. I felt unprepared, having only ever considered negative outcomes. I could hardly believe that what I had always been told was impossible was actually happening. The information vacuum had been punctured and air was rushing in.

The very next day I again received a call from Kate. She spoke rapidly, in an excited tone.

'I've just spoken to your donor and he sounded lovely. I was struck by lots of similarities between how you described yourself and what he told me over the phone. Before settling on medicine, he almost decided to apply for engineering. He said his heritage is a mixture of Anglo-Irish, Scandinavian and Belgian.'

My thoughts were in a whirl. I tried to focus and take in all the new information. Kate explained that the next step was for me to write him a letter. Fresh questions emerged. How long should the letter be? What on earth was I going to say to someone I'd never met before, who was my biological father?

The strangeness of the situation wasn't something I could change, nor something I had asked for. Donor-conceived people seeking information approach these interactions from the back foot, trying to prove themselves worthy of knowing. Our primary concern must always be not hurting anybody else's feelings, rather than expressing our own. I hoped he would agree to meet with me, but felt insecure, acutely conscious of the possibility of rejection.

Like before my meeting with the governor, once again I debated what tone to strike. Should I be formal and factual, or joking and jovial? I knew almost nothing about his personality beyond intuitive deductions from my own. How could I sum up my life in an interesting and non-threatening way, and find out what his feelings were in regard to contact? Worst of all, in the back of my mind I wondered if perhaps in the meantime he'd had a change of heart and would not respond. After getting so far, he could still say no.

In retrospect, I've come to realise that no matter how carefully donor-conceived people word that first contact, the response isn't a reflection of their character, personality, or intelligence. The donor's fear of the nearness (and momentousness?) of the genetic connection, along with their mistrust of the expectations or obligations that might arise from contact, are the critical discomforts that can spoil the attempt to connect.

But after waiting so long there was no time to waste. Fortunately, if there was one thing in the world I knew how to do, it was write. That evening I sat at my desk and began to write a letter by hand. Worried that I might sound a little too earnest, I tried to balance it out with some levity. After finishing, I placed the paper in an envelope and posted it to Kate who was acting as an intermediary. She promised to send it on to my donor. I hoped I hadn't scared him off.

The following week, just as I was about to leave for my Tuesday night netball match I discovered a reply from Kate in the letterbox. I feared that it could be a closed door. It might turn out that he didn't have the same interest and eagerness that I did, and my genetic precariousness was something I would just have to learn to live with. I carried the envelope to my room, but decided not to open it. Perhaps I wanted to luxuriate in the small power of being able to open the letter at a time of my own choosing. I left the sealed envelope lying on my pillow and drove to netball.

When I got back home I sat on my bed, still wearing a black netball skirt and white T-shirt. My face was red and sweaty from the exertion of the game. The envelope made a satisfying tearing sound as I ripped it open. I looked down at what was written on the page and smiled at the strangeness of this loop. Emblazoned across the top of the letter was a name I immediately recognised.

After leaving Chaco Canyon, Gerry and I drove west, away from the sweltering desert, until we reached the San Diego coast. From there, Highway 1 led us north to the restless energy of San Francisco where everything was starting up and nothing slowing down. Our path turned inland to Yosemite, then looped back west over the Sonora Pass and up through northern California. After cutting across the eastern corner of Oregon we crossed the Snake River into Idaho.

This journey was like a pelican; lumbering and awkward in its struggle to get airborne, but so graceful once it managed to take flight. Our days developed a cadence that embodied the simplicity of wellbeing, and the wellbeing of simplicity. On a typical day, Gerry and I awoke to the Sun Dagger spiral on the bedroom wall and jumped down from the mezzanine bed to prepare coffee and fully stacked bagels for breakfast. Mindful of the limited utilities on board the Tan Can, we washed dishes in a cupful of water. After breakfast if we were near a river we walked upstream and plunged into the freezing cold water to float down through the rapids. I would emerge with red, tingling skin; vibrantly awake. We would drive some kilometres on quiet scenic byways, stopping to eat lunch in a shady spot by a lake and maybe go for a swim. The afternoon would be filled with conversation, podcasts and the drive to a camp site where we'd have another swim to freshen up. In the evening I would set up our blue and green camping chairs to face the water and sit reading my book or writing. As hunger grew, I would help Gerry collect pinecones and wood to light a cooking fire in the rock rings at the camp sites. We would eat dinner and split a beer while we watched the sun go down. In the twilight, bats would emerge in erratic flight to feed on insects and moths.

It doesn't sound like a day's activities amounted to much, but endowed with immense wealth in the new currency of time, days no longer passed in a blur. Paradoxically, by doing less each day I felt like I experienced more – a form of radical life extension. The filters that had been dampening my senses were peeled away and, like a return to the wonder of childhood, each day filled me with a volley of sensations: the wind rolling through a wheatfield like a blond-green inland ocean; a kestrel surfing on a stiff breeze displaying mastery in flight. In the evenings I often scribbled intensely in my journal, rediscovering a long dormant love of writing. As time and space continued to open up, I became more and more scripturient – gripped by a violent desire to write.

By camping for free on public land Gerry and I lived cheaply. Our savings went far, as our main outlays were food and petrol. By producing and consuming as little as possible we rediscovered value in the world and ourselves outside the market economy. I noticed the things that made me happy were simple: cooking meals, unhurried walks in nature, thinking and being aware. Sunset watching became a ritual, each occasion unique. Spending less money had the welcome effect of creating fewer expectations and need of status. What had seemed so important – the all-consuming activity of projects and deadlines that had caused us to postpone this trip for several years – gradually fell away. In its place upwelled a tremendous exuberance and sense of freedom from the combination of the vast landscape and the simplicity of travelling light. Gerry felt it too. He wrote, *A beautiful universe awaits only choosing.*

As I slowly rewired to the calm company of trees and water, my mind felt clearer and less distorted, slowly opening up to a new state. I began to catch glimpses of subtler patterns in the landscape: the connection between vegetation and altitude; the rainbow around the sun that signalled that rain was coming. But even amid the peace of the open road there was still that elusive question that I needed to ask myself. I searched for it everywhere – in the ever-changing vista from the windows of the Tan Can, the twinkling stars and within myself – without success.

From Idaho we meandered into Montana and Wyoming. On the morning of 21 August we drove eighty kilometres south of Yellowstone to the Grand Tetons and waited in a field with other sky gazers. Slowly, the air became chilly like night and the quality of the light dimmed to something I had never seen before. The closest analogies were dawn and dusk, but the mountains around me didn't cast the tell-tale long shadows of day's beginning or end. I felt a kind of vertigo, my brain unable to classify what was happening around me.

The eclipse.

Something rare happened in that field. The celestial event overcame mutual distractions and individual concerns as all of us, a group of strangers, synchronised our gaze into single-pointed attention. This unified focus electrified the atmosphere with a sense of expectation.

After a brief flare, day collided with night. I could scarcely breathe for fear of disturbing the balance. The totality. Colour was extinguished and the stars became visible. As the moon passed in front of the sun the corona halo – the sun's crown – became visible. Yet even as it revealed this secret the moon remained a shadowy figure, hidden behind its own darkness.

All too quickly, a cool greenish-gold glow appeared behind the Grand Teton mountains, travelling towards us with vertiginous speed. A blinding diamond flash on the ring of the black void signalled that totality was broken. This also broke the spell of unified focus. The crowds began to pack up their picnic rugs, cameras and tripods. The haste probably reflected a desire to escape the inevitable traffic jams, but I thought it was a shame people couldn't spare a moment to stop and enjoy the second half of the eclipse.

As the sun and moon disentangled, there was a great recovery. The temporarily vanquished sun, shaken from the certainty of its ascendance, emerged victorious from the noon-night. Over the next two hours the grasshoppers and birds gradually resumed their chirping and it slowly warmed up to the usual daytime temperature.

With normality restored, I was left with a childlike feeling of wonder. The midday darkness shook me from a misplaced certainty of how things are, and how they will always be.

The Third Circle

Ten

I stared at the letter in my hand, recognising the name written at the top from the list of Monash medicine graduates I had compiled. Never again did I need to refer to my biological father by the impersonal 'C11'. I had broken the code and he finally had a name.

*Benediction ~ *

A short invocation for divine help, blessing and guidance to promote goodness and wellbeing.

Benedict Manning CLARK

Hello Lauren,

It is all strange as you say, to be connected to someone who is a fully lived adult, and only discover it out of nowhere. Thank you for your letter, very informative, a bit quirky. Sorry about my paper and writing! You said it would be bad! You sound like a smart one! There are a lot of smart people in my family as you can see from the family tree (if you can understand it).

I told the counsellor I used to be keen on engineering and nearly did it at one stage. I had a favourite book – *The Boy Engineer*. I also used to love rockets and space travel. I read lots of books about it and used to design rockets and spaceships of my own. I built some out of fireworks and sent ant astronauts up successfully.

My own interests include medicine – I studied at Monash and am a GP in Wonthaggi and Inverloch. I do anaesthetics and obstetrics as well.

Divorced 2008. 3 children. Charlotte 17
Michael 15
Olivia 14

All in Melbourne. I see them a lot. I also do lots of outdoors things – for an old bloke.

I have 2 horses, fish (Dad used to a lot), surf badly, go on expeditions to NT, WA, Tas hiking. I am interested in reading and art and paint.

Travel – especially to France.

I am lively and withdrawn, depending on mood! Just like my father.

I especially like resting too.

I laughed out loud at this part, as I'm known for falling asleep at opportune moments, or scheduling a nap into my day.

It would be good to hear from you again.

Cheers Ben

Family Tree

My father was,

Manning Clark 1915–1991

Prof of History at ANU. Commentator, annoyer of conservatives, writer.

His father was a Church of England Minister, born in London. His mother was Anglo-Irish.

Medical history of heart disease here. He was also a 1st class cricketer – played for Oxford as wicketkeeper/batsman. Fisherman, avid reader. Very outgoing and witty then shy and gloomy the next. Emotional.

My mother was

Hilma Dymphna Lodewyckx 1916–2000

Mother of 6, very gifted linguist. She won the gold medal for German at Melb Uni. Had an interrupted, almost non-career due to 6 children and the times she lived. Brilliant, very generous but physically aloof. Her father was a Belgian of Flemish background, who became an associate prof of language at Melb Uni. Her mother was Swedish/Norwegian physiotherapist. Cancer in this family.

Their children

Sebastian 1939–

Retired, was a maths teacher

Katerina 1940–

Prof of Russian at Yale University

Axel 1942–2001

Died of cancer. Was an English Lit academic

Andrew 1949–

Journalist, lives in Sydney

Rowland 1955–

Agricultural teacher in Canberra. Part-time farmer and winemaker

Me, Benedict 31/01/1957

I immediately spotted some connections. His family's occupations tallied with my dual interests in writing and mathematics, and I was intrigued to read of Benedict's mother's interest in the German language. My linguistic skills were not nearly as brilliant, but I had been inexplicably drawn to the country and the language. Dymphna's Flemish and Scandinavian background made sense, as my height and hair colour had blended in seamlessly when I travelled through northern Europe.

I was sad to read that Benedict's brother Axel had died of cancer. I remembered the non-identifying information my mother had obtained about C11, including the crossed-out *canc* in the medical history. Maybe that was in reference to Axel?

After reading and re-reading the letter, I left my bedroom and showed it to Mum. As she read she said breathlessly, 'His father was Manning Clark!'

She moved swiftly to the bookshelf and pulled out a book titled *The Quest for Grace* – Manning's autobiography. Flipping through I found photographs of Benedict and his brothers and sister. For the five years I had been searching for C11's identity, the book had sat quietly on the shelf. By coincidence, or cosmic sense of humour, the answers had been there all along.

I didn't know much about Manning Clark but found it apt that after searching so long for my family history, I'd discovered a family of historians. I was thrilled that Benedict described his father as an 'annoyer of conservatives', analogous to Gerry's birthday gift in which he pegged me as an agitator. In time, I came to learn that Manning's magnum opus was the six-volume *A History of Australia*, in which he elevated the inner life of historic figures as important facets of our nation's story. His work explored history through impressions, emotions and meaning, previously absent from a curriculum focused on dates and events. In penning his books, Manning helped transform the dull and dreary subject of Australian history into an animated tale rich in narrative.

Legend has it that Manning wanted to be a novelist, and his books captured the public's imagination. They devoured them, eager to digest their own history and discover their place in the world. Despite this, in later life Manning was accused in some quarters of producing works of creative non-fiction, which projected his own character and spiritual struggles onto the historical figures contained within his volumes.

'Who controls the past controls the future,' observed George Orwell. Intuitively, I understood Australia's history wars, the struggle between earlier histories based on colonial documentation, and later versions, such as Manning's, that brought new perspectives. From my own shock at discovering my dad was not my biological father, I was acutely aware that what we believe to be true can be held in fragile grip.

I wrote a second letter to Benedict with my full name, address and phone number. When he replied he scrawled his address at the top of his letter. Narrowing my eyes, I tried to decipher his doctor's handwriting. He lived in a town I'd never heard of, called Cape Paterson. I searched online and discovered a small hamlet perched on the Bass Coast between Phillip Island and Wilsons Promontory.

A few weeks later, I received a phone call from an unfamiliar number. The caller introduced himself as Ben. Luckily, I didn't have time to be nervous. Annoyingly, the connection cut out no fewer than six times, like the phone network was making a last-ditch effort to keep us apart. Every time we doggedly called each other back, reopening the airwaves. We chatted about our lives, our work and interests. Ben seemed amazingly relaxed about the whole situation. I said I was thinking of coming down to visit him and suggested a weekend in November. He said that would be fine. A few days before the visit he texted that he had told his children and they couldn't wait to meet me.

In the days before our meeting I was wracked by nerves, like I had to prove myself worthy or pass an implicit test. That morning the butterflies in my stomach were too much and I asked Gerry to drive me. Staring out the window at the passing suburbia, I tried not to freak out as Gerry steered us south-east towards Cape Paterson. On a journey with no maps, I nervously twisted my fingers as my thoughts churned. What if he didn't like me? What if I was an unwelcome reminder of the past? What if he just wanted to look at me once, for curiosity, and then cut off contact?

Above Kilcunda the road crested a hill and I momentarily forgot my fears as the view suddenly expanded out over the magnificent Bunurong coastline with an acceleration that felt like escape velocity. Enchanted, I watched blue waves break onto ancient coastal dunes punctuated by six white wind turbines. Then the highway dropped into the town, hugging the coast past the historic rail bridge. Gerry turned right at Wonthaggi and followed the signs towards Cape Paterson.

Height: 5'11"
Hair colour: Fair
Eye colour: Blue

Weight: About 11.5 stone (73 kg)
Race: Caucasian

For years this was all I knew about donor C11, my biological father. Now I wasn't sure what to expect from the real person behind these five non-identifying facts. The hope that I would be liked and accepted was tempered by my self-conscious fear of rejection.

My search for C11 had gone against the grain of social expectations. 'Why do you need to know?' I was constantly asked. 'Your dad is still your dad.' These well-intentioned but ignorant comments from people who had no idea what it was like to be in my position made me feel like an anomaly, as if I were a river that had suddenly chosen to run backwards.

In central Australia, there is a huge interior basin called Kati Thanda or Lake Eyre. In dry years the white salt pan is a great, timeless nothingness – without plants, animals or even shadows – like the unearthly perfection of the idea of who my biological father might be. Now, as I approached the culmination of my search into the past, all I wanted to do was disappear into that perfect void. It would be so easy. No mess, no mistakes, no misunderstandings, no pain, for myself or my family. I wouldn't have to face the reality of the person who lay behind the idea of C11. But the destiny of the dormant salt pan is entwined with the ephemeral lake it will become. As water returns it works a transformation. Barrenness is washed away as the desert explodes into life. And with life comes mess.

Gerry stopped the car outside the address from the letter. My immediate impression was a relaxed beach shack. The house was single storey with a salt-faded wooden verandah wrapped around two sides, encased by a gap-toothed wooden lattice. Large windows opened out onto a view of a clothesline roped to brace a falling-down fence, and the nearby beach.

Heart thumping, with a visceral feeling of staring into the abyss, I said goodbye to Gerry and crossed the threshold by myself. As I walked across the grass I heard a young man call out, 'Lauren's here!' in an excited voice. Immediately, I felt more at ease. Climbing the short staircase to the verandah, I saw the door was open. I walked inside and found myself in a yellow living room, shaking hands with a broad-shouldered man about five foot eleven tall. The bottom button of his 1980s-print shirt was undone.

'Hi, I'm Lauren.'

'Hullo, I'm Ben.'

I couldn't take in everything at once and only managed small glimpses of his face. In his first letter he'd included a couple of photographs, which I'd stared at in fascination. Eventually, I'd realised that Ben was not the man in the foreground of the photos, but half-hidden behind other people. I was unable to integrate those snapshots with the reality of the man who stood before me. Instead, I focused on the living room, which was simply furnished with a wooden table and chairs, an armchair, couch and small television on a wonky stand. The walls were hung with a few oil paintings of the seaside and a print of *Babar à la Neige* – an elephant skiing down the French Alps. My eyes arrived on a tall, broad-shouldered young man wearing a blue T-shirt and navy tracksuit pants – the one who had called out as I walked in. He looked familiar; the masculine version of my long face with prominent cheek and jaw bones, which broke into a bright, friendly smile.

'Hi, I'm Michael,' he said.

'Hi.'

A girl wearing dark-blue leggings and a blue top stood up from the couch. She was a little shorter than me. Her curly blond hair, pulled back into a casual ponytail, was also familiar. She stuck out her hand, nails decorated in bright red polish.

'I'm Olivia,' she said, her smile revealing braces.

'Nice to meet you,' I said, shaking her hand.

'Grab a seat at the table. We were just about to put some things out for lunch,' said Ben.

'I'm vegetarian. I hope that's okay.'

'Of course. Liv is also vegetarian.'

'Really?'

Olivia explained, 'When I was about five years old Michael showed me some animal cruelty videos from PETA.'

'Wow,' I said. 'In high school I did work experience at Animal Liberation, but I couldn't bring myself to watch those videos.'

As I sat down at the wooden table Ben, Michael and Olivia pushed aside a half-empty blue mug and *The Saturday Age* and in their place laid out pita bread, brie and salad.

'Would you like some coffee?'

'Sure.'

Ben switched on the kettle and brought out a French press. After laying everything on the table he poured the coffee and sat down opposite me. I avoided his gaze, and instead turned to my side.

'So what year are you in, Olivia?' I asked.

'I'm going into Year Nine and Michael is going into Year Eleven. Next year I'll be at Howqua, which is a camp for the Year Nines up in the high country near Mt Buller.'

'Oh, cool. Do you get to go skiing while you're up there?' I asked.

'Yeah, that's part of the program.'

'Olivia and I went skiing this winter up at Perisher,' said Ben. 'It was fantastic.'

As he spoke I looked into his eyes for the first time, and unexpectedly located myself reflected back. I sensed a mutual recognition, a flicker of familiarity, like a jigsaw piece falling into place. Being surrounded by strangers who looked like me was surreal. I tried to act normal and not reveal the disconcerting weirdness of carrying on a conversation with someone who was staring back at me with my own eyes.

'I love skiing,' I said, resting my elbows on the table. 'I worked a couple of ski seasons while I was at university, one in the US and one in Canada.'

'Sometimes we go cross-country skiing up at Mt St Gwinear,' said Ben.

'I've never tried cross-country skiing, only downhill.'

'We can let you know next time we're going, if you want to join us?'

'That would be great.'

He still had all his hair, firmly rooted, cut short to reveal a widow's peak around a slightly long face with a heart-shaped jaw and largish nose. Flat eyebrows rested above penetrating blue eyes. His skin was seasoned with the tan of somebody who enjoyed the outdoors, but he didn't have too many wrinkles for an old bloke, just a couple of slight vertical furrows in his cheeks. I recognised his small ears with attached ear lobes.

Michael and Olivia were good-natured and friendly. They chatted a little about their schools and what they'd been up to that year. It was nice having them there, a little relief valve to take the edge off. They lived with their mother and attended school in Melbourne but came back to the beach often on weekends to swim and hang out. As we sat talking, I constantly scanned the mood, checking everything seemed okay.

'Do you guys play any sports?' I asked.

'I started playing Australian Rules Football,' said Olivia.

'Dennis and I play a bit of soccer,' said Michael.

'Who's Dennis?'

'That's what I call Dad.'

'Yes, Michael and I play soccer together. And enjoy fishing. I've also got two horses. My eldest daughter, Charlotte, likes to ride,' said Ben. 'My dad was very competitive in sports. He would pretend he was just playing the game but would hate losing, especially ping-pong. When I was a boy in Canberra we lived close to Parliament House. Bob Hawke used to drop in for a cup of tea until one day Dad trounced him in ping-pong and he refused to come back for a rematch.'

I laughed and Ben grinned. I noticed that Ben, Michael and Olivia all had the same two front teeth; they were a trifle large, taking up the width of three teeth on their lower jaw, just like mine.

'I can relate. I play netball like it's a blood sport,' I quipped. In one of the many surreal moments that day I noticed that Ben and I both had our arms crossed on the table, right over left, holding our elbows, and our legs were arranged in the same way. Was he mirroring my mannerisms, or was I mirroring his? Or was it some sort of expression of genetics?

After taking another bite from his wrap Ben looked at me again. 'You remind me very much of my niece Anna who lives in Sydney.'

I recalled Anna was the daughter of Axel – Ben's brother who had passed away. 'Really?'

'Yes. She studied a PhD too, but in history. How is yours going? Aerospace, isn't it?'

'Yep. Pretty good. I've finished the literature review and started doing some experiments. I'm looking forward to a break over Christmas and January. I want to get out and do some camping with my boyfriend, Gerry. We were thinking of heading to outback South Australia, maybe the Flinders Ranges. It will be pretty hot that time of year, though.'

Ben smiled. 'Some years ago my friend John arranged a hike in the Kimberley over very rough desert tracks. John hikes like a maniac and one of the other guys got sunstroke. That evening he was weak and vomiting. I was a tiny bit worried because we'd been dropped off by boat, and John had arranged a pick-up, but there wasn't any help in between. It was very remote. Luckily, the guy was a bit better in the morning. Everybody else trained in the months leading up to the hike by carrying backpacks full of stones. I said that I trained, but I didn't really. Conveniently, the guy who got sunstroke would ask the others to stop and rest just a moment before I had to.'

I grinned, but below the surface of our casual chat, the whole experience felt liminal and weird. It wasn't about anything Ben, Michael or Olivia had or hadn't said that day. On the one hand it seemed natural, like we had already met. But it also felt a little awkward. The resemblance was so strong, and yet we were strangers – connected in looks, personality and interests, but separated by a complete absence of shared memories.

Professor de Kretser had said that donor insemination had been well established in the United States and proven to be safe, so consequently there was no ethical approval required. I marvelled both at the incompleteness of his understanding of what he had helped set in motion, and the strange loops that had brought me here. Could I lay claim to the parts of myself I saw mirrored in a family that wasn't really mine? At best I was a satellite connected on the strength of genetics. By extension, I questioned my own identity on many levels. The situation wasn't of my choosing, but it couldn't be changed. Sitting here at a wooden table in the house of a stranger, part of the scene, but apart from the others, I again felt a sense that I was an outsider; an unnatural river that had run backwards seeking its source only to reach the inland desert of a wasteland of years.

Why had I lobbed into Ben and his children's lives? What did I want – to alter the cause and effect of decisions made before I existed? It was an impossible and foolish quest. What hope was there for someone like me who had divined meaning from the blank spaces in my life, the pauses between words, redacted codes cut out of records, and things left unsaid, lurking like Dark Emu between the stars of the Milky Way? It was in that moment, sitting opposite Ben, that I finally realised the nature of time. Time was the distance between us – the absence of memories in all the hours spent apart.

'Would you like to go for a walk?'

'Sure.'

Ben, Olivia and Michael walked outside, all barefoot, and I paused to put on my flip-flops, which I'd left at the door. We crossed the road and walked the few metres to the caravan park. A track led through stands of tea-tree and banksia that hugged the dunes to the beach where a boat ramp was set into a curved cove.

'One of the paintings on the wall at home is one I did of Michael at this beach,' said Ben.

'Do you still paint?'

'Not much lately. I haven't had time.'

Walking east along the sandy beach, we passed a natural pool in the rocky wave-cut platform and continued around to Undertow Bay. Taking advantage of low tide, we hopped from one rock to the next around the headland towards the Oaks. Despite their lack of footwear everyone was very nimble on the slippery rocks. They know these beaches. I didn't, and did my best to keep up. Ben slowed down and walked beside me so we could chat.

'Do you fish off these rocks?' I asked him.

'Sometimes. And Michael dives for abalone. My dad was a keen fisherman. He got into it when his family lived at Phillip Island when he was a boy. His father was an Anglican minister posted there for a few years.'

'Do you think your dad was religious?'

'Honestly, I don't think he knew what he was.'

On the way back we bumped into Gerry on the beach and I introduced him to Ben, Michael and Olivia. Together, we walked back to the house and ate berries and cream. As we talked through the afternoon over endless cups of chai with honey I found myself drinking up the tales that Ben recounted.

'One evening when I was about five years old, I didn't come home for dinner. Mum searched everywhere and couldn't find me. Eventually she spotted me sitting high up in a tree. She told me to come down and eat my dinner. Instead, I turned to her and asked, "Mother, why am I mostly so sad?"'

I chuckled.

Gerry and I left in the early evening with a standing invitation to come back for another visit. We gave Olivia and Michael a lift back to Cranbourne station so they could catch the train to their mother's house. As I drove, they dozed. I watched their sleeping faces reflected in the rear-view mirror, heads lolling, mouths slightly open, and thought of how I often fell asleep in vehicles.

Meeting Ben, Olivia and Michael had been strange, tender, familiar and tiring. They were incredibly kind and welcoming as I showed up in their lives, attempting to tease out my tangled identity. The visit had gone well, but I was afraid of it all being ripped away. Maybe they would decide they didn't like me and cut me off. Or maybe, worse, they would just be uninterested. The day had been superficially relaxed, but I was exhausted from the nervous build-up and the mental dance of always trying to put my best foot forward. This is what it's like to be donor conceived; we are constantly questioning and interpreting everything, and nothing can be taken for granted. It's tiring. The four of us hadn't talked about anything too confrontational or serious, but in this game it's not what's said but what remains unsaid that you need to listen out for.

Was my search really over? Was this one meeting enough to know where I came from and who I was? 'Enough is so vast a sweetness, I suppose it never occurs, only pathetic counterfeits,' Emily Dickinson said.

I marvelled at the many strokes of good fortune in the chain of events that had led up to this day. My mother had the courage to tell me the truth; records still existed and a compassionate doctor had arranged the initial contact when the law was unclear; Ben was still alive, had received my letter, and said yes to contact. I was so grateful for all those things, yet somehow amid the gratitude swirled something else that shadowed the gains. What was this feeling that the meeting had been both a comfort and a loss? I patted the pockets of my vocabulary but couldn't turn out anything that seemed appropriate. Maybe it didn't have a name.

A few weeks later I got a phone call from a number that wasn't in my address book. It was Ben's eldest daughter, Charlotte. I was surprised and impressed that she had taken the initiative to call me. After talking on the phone, we made plans to meet in a café near her home in the eastern suburbs of Melbourne. On arrival, Charlotte presented me with a gift of a silk scarf and a card that read, *Dear Lauren, what a wonderful surprise it was to learn about your presence … one can never have enough family, lots of love, Charlotte xoxo.* My heart swelled.

These first meetings did not quite solve the mystery of my identity, but certainly lit a guiding light that got stronger over the years. Yet even as many of the old questions were answered, new ones arose. Was it wrong to spend time getting to know the Clarks as if I was one of them? Was it a betrayal of my dad? Did I really belong, or was I an imposter? Was my family the people I grew up with, or those I didn't know but shared genes with?

I still didn't have all the answers.

A couple of months after this visit Mum and I went to see a movie in Carlton on a Saturday night. It was the same cinema Gerry and I went to on our first date, located just around the corner from the old house in Drummond Street where Mum grew up. After queueing at the box office we were told the movie we wanted to see was sold out. The alternative, a political satire, didn't start for fifteen minutes so we went to a nearby café to have coffee and cake.

As I sat down, I noticed the overhead light illuminate a swirling beam of dust motes. Each speck rode and fell on currents of air, from the air conditioning, the movement of passing people, sound pressure waves, and even perhaps my own breath. I glanced over at the next table and saw two men. One was wearing the same 1980s-print shirt Ben wore on the day we met. It was him. I was conscious that Ben and I were just two more dust motes bobbing through existence as the quantum wave functions of probability that synchronise space and time collapsed. *A million shimmering ripples of cause and effect.*

That night, two months after meeting for the first time, something had brought him two hours from his home in Cape Paterson to Melbourne. In a city of four million people, with endless options for entertainment, we had both chosen to see a movie at the same cinema, at the same time. But it wasn't quite the same time. If the movie Mum and I had planned to see hadn't been sold out we'd already be sitting in the theatre. Or, after our change in plans, we might just have easily browsed the bookstore, or skipped the movie and gone for dinner. Instead here we sat. After all my efforts to arrange my first meeting with Ben, our second encounter arose from us effortlessly ending up three metres from one another.

I leant over and whispered to Mum (this subject always seemed to require secrecy or conspiracy), 'That's Ben sitting there.'

It was her turn to be surprised. 'No, I don't believe it.'

'Yes, that's really him!'

In a daze of instinct I stood up and walked over.

'Hi Ben. What a coincidence!'

He looked up, seemingly unperturbed. 'Oh, hullo. This is my friend John. We're in town for an obstetrics conference.'

Mum came over. I wasn't sure what to do. It seemed appropriate to introduce her. But what was the etiquette for a child introducing her biological parents for the first time? I felt like a ripple in the fabric of spacetime. It's so strange being the answer that came before the question.

'This is my mother, Barbara.'

Mum mumbled a greeting, her face a mask hiding her shock. If they didn't get along, would I disappear in a puff of smoke?

'What movie are you seeing tonight?' I asked Ben cheerfully.

'We're seeing *Bright Star*, about John Keats.'

As we chatted I too wore a mask, doing my best to smooth the interaction behind light-hearted banter. I tried not to think about the fact that I had been created by splicing together the DNA of these two people who I had only moments earlier introduced.

Had my mother and Ben divorced many years ago, like my parents, we might be experiencing a sort of tension that I was familiar with. But the knowledge that I had been conceived from two total strangers manifested as a strangely dehumanising feeling. The scenario was bizarre beyond my grasp. It hurt my brain. As I stood observing the profound disconnection between my biological parents the overwhelming feeling was surreal awkwardness. If they had had any sort of connection, no matter how brief, at least they might have danced together.

I was relieved that it was only ten minutes before Ben and his friend John had to leave because their movie was about to start.

Poor Mum was spun out. 'How do I ever come to grips with having a child with a man I never met?' she asked me later. 'I would like to talk these feelings over with other mothers of donor-conceived children but I've never had the opportunity.'

In retrospect it was probably a good introduction because she didn't have time to be nervous and it was a short meeting, so the awkwardness didn't have to drag on.

Later that evening I tried to articulate my thoughts to Gerry about the chaos of chance and choice that led to that improbable moment.

'What a random universe we live in. Ben doesn't even live in Melbourne. It just goes to prove that something wacky like this can happen. If we hadn't already got in touch and met, which only happened a couple of months ago, there I would have been sitting two tables away from him, and not even known it.'

'Maybe that's already happened.'

'Yeah. Being donor conceived is …' I paused, thinking about how the evening's earnest but awkward meeting between Mum and Ben epitomised the disconnected relationships across the branches of my family tree. 'I mean, going through life knowing there's a chance you're sitting next to a close relative, and not even aware? It's …' I stopped, lost for words.

Ben expressed his own views about our meeting and relationship in an interview recorded by the Infertility Treatment Authority as a resource for other donors who were considering contact:

> I heard about sperm donation when I was a medical student and there was a special appeal made because there was a shortage of donated sperm, so I inquired about it and went ahead. I signed an agreement in response to a request. Hand over sperm, get $10 and get out of there as quickly as possible. I didn't think about it much at the time.
>
> Over the years I used to think about whether anything, or anybody, came of my sperm donations, naturally enough. Particularly because I told a few people I donated sperm and if they spoke about it they always asked if I knew anything and I never did, and so of course you do wonder. I wondered first of all whether there had been any successful pregnancies, births, and what those people were like, and their circumstances. Everything about them, I suppose. It wasn't a very big part of my thinking, I don't think, over the years, but I used to think about it from time to time.

I was a tiny bit surprised when I was initially contacted by Professor de Kretser because I think even though I had thought about it over the years I had almost forgotten about it, to a certain extent, because it was a long time after I donated sperm that I was contacted. I suppose I was curious, and maybe felt the whole thing is just very strange, really. I don't know how to put it exactly. Very strange. It's a bit mysterious. I suppose I didn't really know what to make of it.

I wasn't totally surprised that eventually there was somebody who was interested, that there would be some sort of attempt. Yes, I got a letter from Professor de Kretser and he gave his phone number, and I actually rang him up, spoke to him, and then he told me to get in touch with other people at the ITA – now it's changed its name to VARTA. So, I got in touch with them, through his advice, and found out about what the process was of seeing whether I wanted to make contact with the person who wanted to make contact with me, and went through that process.

So I was given the chance to speak to a psychologist, and did so, and that was good, and made me think about it a bit. I think at that stage I was feeling that it was obviously quite a big effort. Somebody had been born, using my donated sperm, and it wasn't possible, really, for them to contact me, but they made it possible. So I felt at that stage that this was a big effort, so I thought that it would be only fair to make contact with them, for a start, and secondly I thought well if they're that keen, then I think it would be the right thing to do.

I think prior to that I sometimes thought that if somebody wanted to make contact with me I would be a bit ambivalent about it. The thing that changed my mind about whether to make contact with people that had been born through my donated sperm was partly that it was such a big effort to get in touch with me, so it was impressive, I suppose.

The next step was to write letters via an intermediary, and get some information and send off some information myself, and then directly contact this person. Well, she wrote a little explanation about how she had found me, and then she wrote a bit about her own social circumstances and her interests and her family of origin and so on, and especially her interests and also a couple of photographs, and I thought it was interesting that a lot of her interests were similar interests that I've had at various stages. I don't know what that means, but that was interesting, anyway.

So I wrote back to her and sent off some photographs of me and some of my children and also a little potted autobiography, and drew up a family tree, for her interest.

My children knew about the sperm donations, so that was good, because they used to make fun of me about that. They were all really happy about it. They thought it was fantastic and they all wanted to go ahead and meet her. I wrote back to her several times and so we exchanged addresses and phone numbers, and I rang her up and spoke to her a few times and then invited her down to my place. So she came down and had lunch one day, and I had all my children there at the time. I think they were all there. Maybe one was missing, I can't remember exactly.

On the day when we had a meeting I was a little bit … I was really just curious and there was also a bit of a feeling of mystery. And also, there's a funny feeling that there's somebody who is … It's bizarre, the whole thing is bizarre, and I had a feeling of – a little bit of a feeling of having missed out on this person's life, to a certain extent. Or something like that. I'm not too sure what. It's all very odd. Obviously, it's an unusual situation, so it's a bit hard to know how to react to it, but it's basically been very good to meet her, and so on. But it's a bit of a strange situation.

When we had our meeting, it was a little bit odd. She came down and we had a nice time. We just had lunch and went for a little bit of a walk and had cups of tea and biscuits all afternoon, and had quite a lot to talk about. It was good. So it all went very well, really, I think. And I've stayed in touch with her, and met her several times, and been on the phone, which is good.

So I think that my relationship with this person is probably going to be a long-standing one. I'm not too sure what you call it. It doesn't really have a name. I don't think anybody knows what to call it. I really don't know where it is going to go, but I think it will be long-standing. I think we get on very well, we've got a lot in common and we enjoy each other's company and are interested in what's happening in each other's lives, and so on, and also she gets on very well with my children, which is interesting, even though she's older, so that's good. So it doesn't really matter what you call the relationship, because you can't give it a name anyway, so, it will go on. Yeah, it will go on.

Eleven

Setting aside any disappointment that she might have felt about still being without her own answers, Rel was thrilled to hear that I had been able to contact Ben. She had moved to the UK and was taking a break to recover from many long years of lobbying and her unsuccessful search for T5. Busy living her dreams, she had just started a new job as a social worker.

The other TangledWebs members were equally pleased for me, and in their wisdom recognised the complexities of the experience, beyond a simplistic fairytale ending.

Lauren, as you know already, meeting your father will reveal a whole bunch of strong feelings and needs and worries, for you and your family, wrote Romana. It was a relief to spend time with people who knew from personal experience the challenges and shifts in family dynamics that can occur as a result of these reunions. In our regular online and in-person communication, TangledWebs offered me a safe space of support without judgement, which I accepted with gratitude.

I found it outrageous that I had met Ben thanks to the benevolence of the governor, but many donor-conceived people – even those like Rel who were conceived at the same clinic – still had no avenues to find their own biological fathers. Six months after my visit to Cape Paterson, and eighteen months after the Assisted Reproductive Treatment Act had passed by one vote, exactly nothing more had been done about the issue of access to information for donor-conceived people. Despite its promises, the government was stonewalling.

I felt a wave of energy build within me, focused on a sense of injustice about the lack of consistency of the law. Time to agitate. On Myf's suggestion TangledWebs got in touch with the Victorian upper-house Greens member Sue Pennicuik and we arranged a meeting at Parliament House. The TangledWebs representatives were Romana, Myf, me and Kim, another donor-conceived woman who had been through a long and unsuccessful search for information about her biological father.

I found Sue Pennicuik impressive. She used to be an English and physical education teacher, and was both smart and determined. She wore a denim jacket to Parliament House and was the sort of MP who helped clear the stale, male and pale scent out of the place. Myf brought her six-month-old son to the meeting, and Sue delighted in holding him on her knee as she spoke. 'I have believed anonymous egg and sperm donation was wrong since I first heard about it as a teenager in the 1970s. I remember discussing my views with my parents. I take your issue very seriously.'

As a next step, Sue offered to sponsor an information forum at Parliament House to help educate other MPs about the need for change. As I thought about how to help organise this forum I remembered Helen from the ITA's advice that our most effective weapon was our personal stories. I asked Kim if she could speak to the MPs about what it was like to be in her shoes, living life with a hole in her genealogical identity, and she readily agreed.

Next I called Mum.

'I'm helping to organise an information forum at Parliament House next week. I need you to speak from the perspective of a parent about the difficulty in deciding to tell me the truth, because of the limitations of the legislation, and knowing that I could never find out information about my donor.'

'I don't know,' she said. 'I'm nervous about public speaking. And this is such a personal topic.'

I knew it was a big ask, but her presence could make a real impact. I explained it was the kind of compelling story that MPs needed to hear, and she was uniquely placed to tell it. It was important to me, and Mum saw that.

'Okay,' she said in the end. 'I'll do it for you.'

Yet again I experienced nerves that manifested as a terrible sick feeling in my stomach. I tried to control the fear by telling myself to look forward to finally putting the case in front of the real changemakers at Parliament House. This only inflamed the hard knot in the pit of my stomach as I worried about messing up and humiliating myself and the cause. Gardening brought some relaxation, and I tended to beetroot, broccoli, cauliflower and kale growing in my backyard. I also felt a little better when a staff member from Sue's office rang to let me know that there had been some RSVPs. It was a relief to hear that at least somebody was coming.

My PhD was sorely neglected that week as I pulled together the meeting notes. Gerry listened to me practise my presentation, which I hoped would give the MPs an overview of the issues. At the beginning I was awful, and couldn't find the right words to describe the complex situation. But with practice I became more fluent. With Gerry's help I pared down the slides and reduced the amount of text, sticking to the main points and trying to make them as clear as possible. I received Kim's and Mum's speeches and they were both terrific.

The night before, I printed out fifteen copies of the information pack. The volume of my nerves increased. When I finally got to bed, I snuggled into Gerry's warmth. Conscious of time, conscious of self, somehow I managed to block out thoughts of the next day and mercifully went to sleep.

The morning of the information session, a Thursday, Mum, Gerry and I caught the bus into the city. I knew Mum had dressed up because she wore her clip-on earrings. We climbed the imposing steps of Parliament House to where Kim sat, practising her speech to her sister, Kylie. When she was ready, we passed through the huge Doric columns guarding the entrance. After we cleared the metal detector, the security guard gave us 'V' stickers to wear.

'V must stand for Victory,' I joked.

Sue arrived slightly after us. She'd left her denim jacket at home and wore a tailored brown blazer instead. She led us to the Legislative Council Committee Room, which was decorated with dark polished-wood panelling and chandeliers hanging from the four-and-a-half-metre ceiling. A projector had been set up for us, and there were four rows of black leather chairs for the attendees.

I was prepared for anything – except the obligatory last-minute technology failure. The projector wouldn't connect to my laptop. Gerry and I tried everything, but there was just a blank, blue screen, mocking all the work I had put into my presentation. We had arrived early but as the minutes ticked by things got more and more tense.

By this time all the MPs had assembled and were starting to look antsy, checking their phones. Some made furtive eyes for the door. Sue took me aside and said, 'Listen, we're out of time. Just talk to the MPs directly, without the presentation.' Sue's steady gaze transmitted a beam of belief and confidence into my faltering demeanour. 'I know you can do this, Lauren.'

I took a deep breath. The show must go on. 'Okay. Let's do it.'

Mentally I tried to translate the printed copy of my slide notes into a direct speech, but then a small miracle occurred. An IT staffer on the phone gave Gerry some technical advice that worked. I took a few more deep breaths as Sue began the forum with some introductory remarks, keeping the MPs' attention for the painful few minutes it took my crappy second-hand laptop to boot up.

Finally the laptop loaded. On the white screen flashed the text:

Sue Pennicuik MLC
Member for Southern Metropolitan Region
Presents a forum about:
The ongoing issues for donor-conceived people,
after the *Assisted Reproductive Treatment Act 2008*

Sue handed over to me and I stepped up to the lectern. As I looked out at the audience I was pleased to see that almost all the chairs were full. All my nerves vanished and a killer instinct kicked in.

'Thank you all so very much for attending this forum exploring the ongoing issues for donor-conceived people after the Assisted Reproductive Treatment Act. My name is Lauren Burns and I am a donor-conceived person.'

As I summarised my personal story, I sought out familiar faces in the audience. There was Louise, CEO of the Victorian Assisted

Reproductive Treatment Authority (VARTA), which was the successor of the ITA. There was also Denis and Gary, the chair and the manager of the Victorian Adoption Network for Information and Self Help (VANISH), both of whom I knew from volunteering on their committee of management. Rel was still in the UK but TangledWebs was well represented by the powerhouse duo of Myf and Pauline, steadfast as ever. Buoyed by their presence and support, I started making eye contact with the various MPs as I recapped the current three-tiered legal system.

'People conceived from gametes donated prior to 1 July 1988, including myself and Kim, who you will hear from soon, have no access to identifying information about our donor parent. People conceived from gametes donated between 1988 and 1997 can access the identity of their donor parent as long as the donor consents to the release of this information. People conceived from gametes donated after 1998 have an unqualified right to access the identity of their donor parent.'

The preparation paid off as I spoke without ums or ahs, hardly glancing down at my notes.

'Relax,' Gerry had said to me during the practice run-through that morning. 'You know this stuff inside out.'

I continued. 'The main problem with this three-tiered legislative system is some donor-conceived people are more equal than others, which creates a conflict with natural justice or procedural fairness. If, as the law says, it is essential that every donor-conceived person born today has the right to know where they come from, then why shouldn't everybody have this right?

'As it stands there is a conflict with the government's own Time to Tell campaign, which encourages parents of donor-conceived people to tell their children the truth, because the law makes no provision to answer the questions that will inevitably follow. This puts parents in a very difficult position, as you'll hear more about later from my mother, Barbara.

'There is a further conflict with the first guiding principle of the Assisted Reproductive Treatment Act, which states, "the welfare and interests of persons born or to be born as a result of treatment procedures are paramount". Note, the word used in the legislation is "paramount", meaning above all others.

'I'm also very concerned about the pre-1988 donor records, which are unprotected, and could legally be destroyed at any time. They need to be preserved.'

I noticed a few MPs nodding in agreement. Spurred on, I finished laying out the legal and moral arguments. 'Finally, individual clinics and doctors are already being approached by pre-1988 donor-conceived people and being forced to make policy decisions about whether to contact donors, without guidance from legislation. This results in inconsistencies. For example, Melbourne IVF has a policy of contacting pre-1988 donors on request, whereas other clinics, such as Monash IVF, do not. Some clinics, such as Prince Henry's Hospital where I was conceived, have closed down and the records are orphaned. The end result is people are being discriminated against not only depending on *when*, but also *where* they were conceived. Guidance from legislation is required to standardise outcomes.'

Next I introduced Kim. She stepped up to the lectern and pulled out a printed copy of her speech. Sweeping a lock of dark hair away from her eyes, she began speaking in a quiet but steady voice.

'I am a donor-conceived adult born in 1984. My older brother, Jeff, and sister, Kylie, are also both donor conceived. I came to learn the truth about this early in 2005. At the time I was twenty-one years old. It was my half-sister, twenty-two years my senior, who revealed the long-held secret; our father was not genetically related to us. Furthermore, our biological father had donated his sperm anonymously to create us.'

Kim went on to explain that her half-sister did not make the decision lightly, but their sister, Kylie, had been suffering from some medical issues, and her doctor was adamant there must be a genetic factor.

'It was at this point that the decision to tell us the truth became unquestionable, as it clearly impacted on our health and wellbeing.'

Kim detailed the waves of shock and devastation triggered by the revelation, which were compounded by her powerlessness in finding out that legally she had no rights to information. She felt a further trauma after contacting the clinic where she was conceived, Monash IVF, which dismissed her inquiries, saying they had no record of her biological father's identity.

'After just over three years of silent grieving I thought to myself, "This isn't fair. This is my life and my history." Not only does this history belong to me, but also to my children and our family. I contacted the Infertility Treatment Authority and spoke with an extremely empathetic woman who endeavoured to help me. She corresponded with the clinic to try and find out more information. To my utter shock she was able to discover that the name of my biological father was in fact somewhere on the file! Suddenly I had hope. I had also developed a deep distrust of the clinic, who instead of fulfilling their moral obligation to help me, chose to do the opposite.

'Despite the fact that a name had been found on my biological father's file, the clinic refused to facilitate any exchange of information. I was not asking them to provide me directly with identifying information, simply to make contact and let him decide for himself if he wished to help his genetic children put together the pieces of their history. Unfortunately, I am still searching.

'People need to know their genetic history and family in order to find their place of belonging in the world. This doesn't just affect me. It impacts on my kids. These issues are intergenerational.'

One of Kim's children had been diagnosed with a serious medical condition that is known to be partly genetic. She was raising her kids while also working in childcare. Yet, despite all these responsibilities, she had taken the time to write her speech and travel from Belgrave to the city centre to deliver it in person. I glanced anxiously at the faces of the assembled MPs and hoped they were listening.

'These days children created from donor conception have their rights protected by law. Upon adulthood they can access information about their biological parents and family. They are able to piece together the genetic puzzle of their lives. This right has not been fully extended to donor-conceived people born before 1998 and not at all to those born before 1988, yet it is just as important for us to know.

'I believe there is an inner desire in every one of us to seek out our roots. Some of us are fortunate enough not to have to search very hard. Donor-conceived people need the basic right to information about their genetic identity. We are subject to emotional, mental and physical suffering. And without it we continue to search.'

Kim sat back down beside her sister, Kylie. They held hands and wept silently together.

I handed over to Mum to bring us home. It was time to break the silence and say those words that she hadn't been able to speak aloud for over twenty-five years. Time to be free of the burden of secrets. Time to tell the politicians her story. I could tell she was nervous. Her expression looked oddly familiar, like that hazy summer day when she called me over to the sofa to tell me her secret. Eyes downcast, hands shaking. Steely determination. She stood up and approached the lectern. With her glasses perched on the bridge of her nose, she spoke slowly and deliberately, reading from the printed copy of her speech.

'I want to tell you as a parent why the law on donor-conceived children having access to information about their donor must be examined. After nearly a quarter of a century of keeping the secret, in 2005 I told Lauren that she was donor conceived.'

In my mind's eye I pictured the uninvited guest who joined us after that conversation. How could any of us have known all that would happen to bring those blurry features into the light?

'She was conceived prior to the arbitrary cut-off date of 1988, before which she is officially not permitted to know anything about her donor. I thought about it for a long time before actually getting the courage to speak. A major influence in telling was the fear that she would find out accidentally. I had a horror of Lauren, many years down the track, being involved with her social father's medical treatment and suddenly realising that his blood type or DNA was incompatible with her own, and that she had been lied to all her life. I believe with the discoveries in genetics and medicine this will become a regular scenario and many donor children will be placed in this shocking situation. This in itself is a compelling reason why out-of-date laws about who can or cannot have information must be changed. By not addressing the issue now we are heaping up trouble for the future.

'The other strong argument for change is that when I was contemplating telling, I was aware that Lauren was not legally entitled to any information about her donor. It seemed almost a sick joke to have to admit to my child that they were conceived by a stranger whom they would never know anything about.'

Mum looked up from her printed page for the first time to make eye contact with her audience.

'Neither I nor anyone else should ever be placed in that position.'

She looked back down.

'I also want to mention what I think is the main impediment in most people's minds about removing the secrecy. That is the fear factor. Will parents and donors be upset and feel let down by the removal of a law that promised them secrecy? I am a parent, and I would not be upset but would be very happy to see the law changed. Yes of course I did have some anxiety over this journey – it is not easy stuff – but I am absolutely convinced that the only way forward is to tell the truth and remove all barriers to providing information.

'As you have heard, Lauren did eventually find her donor against very long odds, by essentially battling against the system in a David and Goliath struggle that a lesser person would not have been able to undertake, let alone win. Her donor has been wonderful and, now that the dust has settled, we have all reached a new and better reality. My family and friends have been most supportive. Surely we are a normal case, and our experience is likely to be typical of many other normal people in the same situation. Providing information on donors is not breaking new ground. It is merely the last in a continuum. The sky did not fall on adoptees and their parents when the legal situation changed. Society has accepted openness, as evidenced by the popularity of programs like *Find My Family*. What surprises me is that the same battles have to be fought again and again.

'Finally, I believe that a person has an absolute right to know their biological origins and genetic heritage, and that I and the government are cheating them if we do not have the courage to do all in our power to give them this information. The way forward is for unresolved donor-conception issues to go to the Law Reform Committee. It is up to you. Through coming here today I know you are listening. Thank you.'

I smiled at Mum as she sat down. I felt so proud of her for writing and delivering such a persuasive speech. Speaking in front of a roomful of politicians at Parliament House about something so deeply personal and private really pushed her out of her comfort zone. But she had overcome her fears. Not just that; she had absolutely nailed it. There was redemption in her language of love.

Finally, Sue stood up and could hardly speak as she blinked back tears, thanking everybody for attending.

Afterwards I mingled over food and drinks, trying not to drop the hors d'oeuvres down my top. Some MPs made comments about the need to protect the remaining donor records immediately. Denis Napthine talked about being involved in drafting the standing legislation fifteen years earlier and how concerns about donors had stopped them going the whole way towards freedom of information, but that now he believed it was time for review. Jenny Mikakos said it wasn't a done deal that the government would support the motion. The discussion went for twenty minutes, until the bell clanged and the MPs scurried off like schoolchildren.

Pauline sought me out to give me a present and a card. Security were kicking us out so I put the gift in my bag, together with some leftover sandwiches from the catering. Walking outside, I felt like a tremendous weight had been lifted off my shoulders. We stopped and Gerry took a photo of Mum, Kim, Kylie and me on the steps of Parliament House, which didn't seem quite so imposing as they had that morning.

On the bus home I unwrapped Pauline's present. It was a biography of Manning Clark by Mark McKenna, titled *An Eye for Eternity*. The card read:

> Dear Lauren,
>
> Your grandparents' remarkable contribution to the history of Australia lives on through you; their grandchild. We are so proud of you!
>
> Pauline and Gordon Ley.
>
> On the occasion of your presentation at Parliament House, Melbourne.

Later, reading this biography, I discovered the Clark family had form in welcoming unexpected members who showed up out of the blue. One day, Manning was visited at home in Canberra by a woman named Margaret. He was astonished to discover she was his half-sister. Their father, an Anglican minister, had an extramarital affair with his housekeeper, which had resulted in Margaret's birth. Despite the shock, she was quickly embraced as 'Auntie Margaret'.

After the information forum, Sue's motion to hold an inquiry into information access for donor-conceived people passed in a unanimous vote. But before the inquiry began there was a state election, putting the more conservative Liberal Party in power. Still, the brand-new government appointed five cross-party members to the Law Reform Committee and referred the inquiry, titled 'Access by Donor-Conceived People to Information about Donors', to them. The committee began by inviting public comment.

Around this time, the ITA counsellor Kate Bourne linked me to a man named Ian who had been a sperm donor at Prince

Henry's Hospital in the mid 1980s. We met for coffee and clicked immediately, spending hours trading stories about our experiences on different sides of the donor-conception triangle. In the late 1990s Ian had received an unexpected letter from Monash IVF, which had absorbed the Prince Henry's clinic. It had been sent to a much older address but Australia Post had doggedly forwarded it until it reached his current residence. The letter informed Ian that he has seven donor-conceived children. As he puts it, 'I am the biological father of nine children. Two of my offspring live with me, and seven I have never met.'

Ian joined TangledWebs and soon began lobbying for the law on donor anonymity to change. It was incredibly powerful when he wrote letters and attended meetings and could answer questions from politicians about why he – a donor who had been promised anonymity – supported the proposed legislative changes.

Another person who arrived at just the right time was Professor Sonia Allan, a legal academic and expert in health law and regulation. She edited a special edition of the *Journal of Law and Medicine* on the proposed law change, pulling together some of the best legal minds to examine issues raised by the prospect of removing donor anonymity. In her submission to the Law Reform Committee she proposed a model whereby donors could stipulate how much contact they wanted via legally enforceable contact preferences. Separating out information release from unwanted contact was a masterstroke that helped address the single largest objection to reversing anonymity – what to do about donors who wished to maintain their privacy.

I continued to try to advocate and educate. Kate Bourne organised for Helen, David de Kretser, Mum and me to speak on a panel about donor linking at the Fourteenth World Congress on Human

Reproduction. On the appointed day I walked through the trade show in the Melbourne Exhibition Centre past a bewildering array of booths spruiking their wares.

> Eggs deserve the best!
> Cross Border Fertility Solutions: Worldwide egg donation and surrogacy
> Diverse donor pool
> Top pregnancy success rates
> Cost savings of up to 40%
> Money back guarantees

Nearby, a digital counter scrolled on a large LED screen, clocking over to 1,000,011. Underneath it was written, *1 million babies and counting.*

Damian from TangledWebs was a friendly face in the audience during the panel discussion. Apart from him the audience was mostly made up of infertility counsellors, the majority women, possibly encouraged by Kate, who was their association president. I knew Gab Kovacs – former head of the Prince Henry's donor insemination service – was at the conference because I had glimpsed his face among the throng in the trade show. He didn't attend Kate's session to listen to his old colleague David de Kretser speak about donor linking. In fact, there were hardly any doctors in the audience. They didn't seem interested in a presentation focused on stories of human experience. Perhaps their scientific training couldn't countenance the validity of what the people they had created had to say about the social impacts of their scientific research. After all, our lived experiences aren't underpinned by the gold standard of double-blind experimental trials.

The chasm between my and Gab Kovacs's perspectives was the difference between knowledge and understanding. Doctors operate in a world of knowledge: verifiable and scientific, like the five non-identifying facts about C11 disclosed to me, which contained nothing of his essence. Donor-conceived people inhabit a world of understanding, based on what it feels like to live our lives.

Perhaps Gab Kovacs didn't attend because he was of the view that there was nothing wrong with non-disclosure because it wasn't harmful. In 2015 he published a paper titled 'Keeping a Child's Donor Sperm Conception Secret Is Not Linked to Family and Child Functioning during Middle Childhood: An Australian comparative study'. His methodology to justify this title involved surveying mothers who had received donor-conception treatment at Prince Henry's Hospital who had children aged between five and thirteen.

I find it extraordinary that ethical approval was granted to conduct research on children whose parents had not told them they were donor conceived, meaning they were unaware they were participating in the study. Kovacs asked mothers who had chosen not to disclose the truth to their children to appraise whether there were any problems for the child or family as a result of this decision. The study found that mothers reported there were no issues, and Kovacs appeared widely in the media promoting its results. He never followed up his research with another study addressing the obvious unanswered question: what is the impact of late or accidental disclosure on donor-conceived people and their families? Nor has he ever undertaken any research studies that directly interviewed adult donor-conceived people, rather than their parents.

The evening after the eclipse I flipped through our paper road atlas to the map of Utah. With my finger I traced the blue line of the Green River north as it rewound up into Wyoming towards its origin in the Wind River Range. I felt a force drawing me there, like a magnet. A secret part of me hoped that tracing the source, not too distant from our present location, would provide a resolution to the mysteries I had encountered on the river.

Steering south, we reached the small town of Pinedale nestled under the serrated horizon of the Continental Divide. The Green River's headwaters lay hidden somewhere within the heart of the looming mountain range, its jagged granite peaks in sharp relief against the blue sky.

In town Gerry and I revictualled and packed our backpacks. After dinner and a beer at the brew pub we drove thirty minutes out of town on a dark, pot-holed road to find the trailhead. The remainder of the journey would have to be on foot. Curling up in our mezzanine bed beneath the Sun Dagger spiral, I again tried to remember the urgent question on the tip of my tongue. But, as I fell asleep, it remained elusive.

The next morning Gerry and I shouldered our backpacks, carrying our needs for the next four days, pared back as much as possible: one set of clothes, plus a couple of extra warm items; one tent; two mattresses and sleeping bags; an alcohol stove; fuel; and food. Everything we carried was essential. With nothing extra to weigh me down, I felt free.

We set off and the trail climbed steadily uphill for several kilometres through a forest of spruce and fir. It emerged onto a flat plateau of rock, revealing lakes in every direction: blue, green, rippled, still, silt bottomed and clear. We stopped briefly for lunch, then continued uphill following a stream. Over the clattering of our footsteps on granite, I heard the high-pitched bleats and whistles of pikas and marmots. I was sharply awake, senses alert, with a feeling of strength in my body.

As Gerry and I climbed higher the vegetation morphed from forest into low alpine scrub, punctuated by carpets of wildflowers in the boulder-strewn grassy meadows. Delighting in the fragrance, I noticed that as we gained elevation the plants rewound from empty open seed pods, to closed seed pods, to the height of their flowering. Perhaps it really was possible to go back in time.

The green mist of vegetation swept up the valley and disappeared into the steep, rocky faces of the mountains. Dark stains of past waterfalls, like desert varnish, discoloured the cliffs. We took a col tucked between two talus-covered slopes. 'What a view!' I exclaimed to Gerry as we crested the pass. Over the other side lay a vast lake shaped like a long, blue mirror with an island at its centre. It rested at the foot of the Wind River Range, which appeared before us like a procession of dinosaurs standing tip to tail. Locating the source of the Green River meant finding a way through the steep scree fields and hanging glaciers to penetrate deep into the foreboding range. Those peaks were like locked gates guarding their secrets.

The trail descended through fields of rocky shale towards the lake. A palette of green, orange and red lichen overlaid splashes of colour onto the greyscale granite boulders dabbed with patches of white snow. The path meandered uphill again for several kilometres past a chain of clear, snow-fed lakes. The petrified ground became even rockier, as though Medusa had passed by. Eventually a basin came into view, housing twin lakes tied together by an umbilical of cascades. Hopping across a series of rocks we crossed the upper cascades and reached spongy level grass to pitch our tent.

I unfolded the map. Our camp site was situated at the end of the dashed line marking the trail. Looking up, I felt intimidated by our intended route up into the steep glacier-studded mountains that lay ahead.

'What do you think?' I asked Gerry.

'Let's just try,' he suggested.

The twin lakes were still, reflecting the last vestiges of the day. After dinner I walked a short distance to sit cross-legged by the waterfall on a contour of polished rock.

There's something intensely satisfying in watching water flow in all its myriad forms: drumming rain, winding rivers, seeping springs, or a glacier flowing down a valley. Dusk darkened to lavender grey and the waning moon, just past full, bathed the buttresses of the peaks in silver. In the thin atmosphere the temperature quickly plummeted. Returning to camp I crawled into a nest of sleeping bags and drifted off to sleep listening to the soft, comforting gurgle of water, gathering strength for what lay ahead.

Twelve

Rel wasn't at the human reproduction conference because she was still living and working in London. A few months later, in the autumn, she returned home to Melbourne. Not long afterwards Myf called to tell me that Rel had woken up with stomach pains so severe she had been rushed into surgery. The operation found the source of her agony was a perforated bowel. I could hardly believe my ears as Myf explained that Rel's bowel had been punctured by a large tumour. Even worse, the tumours had already spread to Rel's lungs and liver. Unthinkably, at age twenty-eight, Rel had just been diagnosed with stage-four bowel cancer.

For years Rel had blogged about being donor conceived under the moniker 'T5's daughter'. She had been open about her journey with donor conception and her approach to cancer was no different. Rel relayed via her blog that the doctors had explained to her that chemotherapy was for 'life extension' rather than cure. Stage four was a terminal diagnosis. But in announcing the doctor's prognosis she also made clear her plan to defy the odds and survive. Isn't transcending our limited circumstances what humans do?

In subsequent weeks Rel posted videos documenting her course of chemotherapy, filming the doctor insert a shunt into the delicate skin near her collarbone. Her iconic long, brown dreadlocks endured the potent drugs without falling out. After beginning chemotherapy the first scans showed positive results. The tumours had shrunk under the force of the chemical onslaught. I knew that if anybody could defy the odds, it was Rel.

Indeed, Rel showed the rest of us not just how to survive, but how to live. After her emergency surgery she had to contend with a colostomy bag but, undaunted, she travelled to the US to take part in Burning Man festival in the Nevada desert. She also kept dating, determined to find a pure and unconditional love to break the cycle of fear and abandonment that she had told me about years before. I was touched by her courage.

In the spring the Law Reform Committee convened a series of public hearings in which interested parties could talk directly to the committee. Despite all her appointments and regular hospital admissions for chemotherapy, Rel was determined to testify. We were scheduled to speak on the same day and we made our way to the Legislative Council Committee room together, finding two empty seats next to each other. Also present to give evidence were Helen and another woman, called Rita, who worked as a counsellor for Monash IVF.

At the appointed time Rel stood and, with careful movements that underlined her fragility, walked to the presenting table and sat down. She slowly unfolded a slip of paper and began her testimony.

'My name is Narelle Grech. I'm here today because I've got something to say. I wanted to thank you, firstly, for allowing me this opportunity to speak. I'm twenty-nine and I've known about my donor-conceived status since I was fifteen years old. I was conceived by an anonymous sperm donor whose donor code is T5, so that's what I will refer to him as. He donated at Prince Henry's in the early 1980s. Since this time, since learning about my donor conception, I've wanted to access my records, so it's been fourteen years that I've been seeking this information and it's been quite a journey.'

The woman recording the proceedings typed furiously on her shorthand machine as the five members of the Law Reform Committee focused on Rel.

'What happened when you first sought that information?' asked the chair, Liberal MP for Prahran Clem Newton-Brown.

'I made an initial contact with Professor Kovacs, who was my mum's treating doctor, and he sent a letter, after accessing search support services through VANISH, which is the adoption support agency. They helped him to send a letter to three people in the phone book, I believe it was, with the same first initial and surname as T5. Nothing ever came of that. I made a further request a few years later for another attempt at contact and that was actually denied. Professor Kovacs said that the ethics board from Prince Henry's, which is now Prince Henry's Research Institute – they said that they didn't believe it was okay to make more than one attempt due to privacy. I've requested to see the letter that was initially sent but never received that so there's been a lot of inconsistency in my search.

'What I do know about my donor, or T5, from the non-identifying information is that he was a student at the time and he was married. He had brown hair and brown eyes, his blood group was O positive and I was told his height and weight at the time of donation. I was also able to learn years later that his surname starts with the letter T, and is most likely of Maltese origin. This would make sense as both of my parents are Maltese and the clinic would have tried to match him with my dad.

'I'm not going to go into great detail today about my story, as I've written about it quite extensively in both of my submissions. I've been actively speaking out about donor conception for a number of years, and it's taken its toll on me emotionally and within my family. It's personally quite taxing to have to recount my story and to have to plead for information that I feel I should already have. The lack of control around this is very disempowering; the secrecy and withholding of information about who I am and my conception leads me to feel like a second-class citizen.'

Hearing Rel testify brought back my feelings of relief when we first met, in finding somebody who understood exactly how I felt.

'I believe that the truth will set me free, so to speak, and I ask for access to my records for this reason. I want answers so that I can move forward in life without these feelings of loss and grief. I don't think anyone should have to endure this, especially when the records do exist. And I do know that my records exist.'

'How do you know your records exist?' asked Clem.

'Because Professor Kovacs has told me that he has them, he has access to them – like, to do the search initially – and I believe they were at one point held at the ITA.'

'And your biological father said no?' asked the deputy chair, Jane Garrett, Labor MP for Brunswick.

'I haven't had any response at all. There was one attempt made when I was fifteen, and we made that inquiry quite soon after I found out,' said Rel. 'I'm definitely not only speaking out for myself but also for other donor-conceived people who are unable to make their voices heard for whatever reason. And I feel that if it weren't me, or the small group of us that are doing this, then – who would be speaking out? So I feel very compelled to tell my story and this is why I have done so for so many years. I have felt like I don't have any choice because this has been my path.'

Rel's words struck a chord in me: the feeling of having no choice, of walking the path you're confronted with.

'Donor conception is the reason I decided to go on to study social work. During this time I learnt about a theory called "disenfranchised grief", which is a theory that Kenneth Doka put forward, and I wanted to speak a little bit about that because it has some relevance to where I'm at. He defines it as: "Grief that persons experience when they incur a loss that is not or cannot be openly acknowledged, publicly mourned or socially supported." I think this theory applies to myself and other donor-conceived people because I can't publicly mourn the loss of my biological father and my paternal family as I already have a dad, who society regards as being all that I need.

'My biological father is labelled as my donor, and I believe this blurs the true relationship between us. We are socially viewed to have no relationship, and therefore I should not feel a loss, but I do feel a great loss for the severed ties for my paternal family. I'd love to know who they are, what we share in common, who I've inherited certain traits from, not only physically but in terms of my personality, and this is knowledge most people take for granted.

'I can't publicly mourn my loss because, as I said, the relationship isn't recognised. No-one has actually passed away so there's no socially acceptable way for me to mourn the loss of my father, his family or for myself, and I'm not socially supported. In voicing my grief I've been met with a lot of negative feedback over the years. I think it was really quite difficult in the early days – I've been speaking about this since about 2003 – and initially I was met with a lot of negative feedback. For example, I must be ungrateful, that I was being disrespectful towards my parents who raised me, and that obviously I was doing this because I had a bad childhood and therefore was looking to replace my dad or my parents. And I wanted to say that this is not the case at all. So, using Kenneth Doka's theory, you can begin to see how not being able to know my paternal family and my biological father has impacted on me over the years.

'With regards to my eight half-siblings, there are three girls who were born the same year as me. I was able to find out this information a few years later doing some more detective work. Three boys born the year following and two girls born in 1985. I consider them to be my family, and I feel a loss for not being able to know who they are.'

Rel explained some of the detective work that had been required to track down her siblings, and Clem listened closely.

'What would be the process now if you were to start your search from scratch?' he asked. 'I know you went to Professor Kovacs originally.'

'I'm trying to again through Professor Kovacs. He called me today actually, and that was an interesting conversation, because he's now saying he has to clarify that my donor code is T5. I think it was quite unprofessional of him to say that now he has to check that my donor code is T5, when for me that's been a huge piece of information for fifteen years – the only name I've ever known for my biological father. I was quite upset – and this is the kind of thing that happens all the time.'

The Law Reform Committee chair, Clem, turned to Rita, the counsellor from Monash IVF.

'Rita, you could be in a situation where donor-conceived children contact you and you assist them with Prince Henry's records, is that right?

'Yes. We have some of the Prince Henry's records.'

'How would you deal with Narelle's situation if she were to contact you and ask for your assistance?' asked Clem.

'I have,' interjected R[illegible]el

'I think we locate whether those records exist,' said Rita. 'If they exist within that particular doctor's private collection, which it sounds like they might, that's a different issue. So there are some Prince Henry's records that exist within the clinic, that they have access to, and the doctors themselves working at Prince Henry's at that point in time have kept their private records.'

'So the hold-up in this situation is the doctor himself?' asked Clem.

Helen interjected. 'What also exists is a file at ITA, so I don't know what happened with that. Many of the donor-conceived records actually came to ITA, and they include the details of who the donor is. But it was not information that ITA were going to act upon, because we were advised legally that we were unable.'

'Because what, sorry?' asked Clem, confused.

'We were legally unable. The information was there but because Kovacs was the private doctor who treated Narelle's mother – he had done that before ITA, before the donor registers were actually created, and he'd done that as a private doctor, which was absolutely his right – but ITA had no capacity at all because it was pre 1988,' explained Helen.

Inwardly, I rolled my eyes at the wheels of complexity and confusion spinning around the room.

'What would need to be changed for ITA to release that information?' asked Clem.

'You would legally need to make contact with the donor,' said Helen.

'Which again goes back to the point – is that based on the agreement that private clinicians had with the donors?' asked Jane.

'It's pre 88—,' began Helen, but Jane interrupted her.

'I know it's pre 88 but the committee's already heard that Monash and Melbourne IVF are now contacting pre-88 donors.'

'That's because there's a private doctor to go to,' said Helen.

'That's right. So it's about the private doctor.'

'It sounds like there also needs to be some framework around the manner of invitation or how often you invite people to contact,' said Clem. 'Professor Kovacs has sent letters some years ago; is that right?

'Yes, when I was fifteen,' replied Rel.

'How old are you now?'

'Twenty-nine.'

'So it seems like there should be some sort of framework around if you've been contacted three times and five years has elapsed and maybe you've changed your mind and it's appropriate to send another letter.'

'Yes. I tried to make a further inquiry when I was about twenty-one and Professor Kovacs said that he consulted the ethics board of Prince Henry's Institute of Research and that they decided that not more than one attempt at contact could be made, and that's what I had to deal with. But I don't agree that only one attempt being made is enough. I did ask Professor Kovacs to see a copy of the letter he sent, because I would even query what he'd written, whether he consulted a counsellor, even. That the letter itself may have been, I don't know, off-putting. I query whether he actually did that search. I don't have a lot of trust in the doctors. I don't have a lot of trust in the system. I've been lied to from the time of my conception – so why should I believe that anything has been done now? I feel a big lack of control and mistrust.'

I understood how Rel felt. The question of trust was so crucial, and it had been betrayed over and over by the people who had claimed to have our best interests at heart.

'And the other thing is, when I found out, I wasn't at all offered any counselling. There were no provisions for that, and I had to deal with it on my own. And I did for quite a number of years. I saw a school counsellor, but they had no idea about donor conception. I did end up seeing one counsellor, a fertility counsellor, when I was about eighteen, but I was the first donor-conceived person she had met. She'd only ever spoken with infertile couples. She helped me a little bit but I had to support myself through it.'

'Do you know if the doctor has contacted your siblings?' asked Clem.

'No, I don't think he has. I have put my information onto the Voluntary Register in hopes of finding anyone, be it the donor or the half-siblings. I would be interested to know them or meet them, or even exchange information through the register.'

'Half-siblings would have to have done what you've done, and gone back to finding the treating doctor?'

'Exactly. And they would have to know they were donor conceived. I'm relying on the fact that their parents have told them and I'd say that most of them don't know that they're donor conceived because it's not reflected on the birth certificate, and that makes me very angry. I could go my whole life without knowing any of them. I could meet them in the street. I could have met them already. I do go on to speak about that, if I can continue with my submission. I feel very strongly that all donor-conceived people need to know the truth about their conception.

'I've gone to strange and great lengths to search for T5. This is a little bit embarrassing. I had a dream years ago that T5's surname is Aberdeen. I was so moved by this dream that I sent letters to all the Aberdeens in the White Pages in Melbourne asking if they had donated sperm at Prince Henry's. Unfortunately, I only received letters back stating that they were not who I was looking for. You might think this is a very strange thing to have done but when you have little or no information you're forced to follow your heart.

'I feel like I've been dealt a dud hand for so many reasons. Not only do I not have access to my records, earlier this year on 2 May my whole life was turned upside down. I was diagnosed with stage-four bowel cancer following an emergency surgery at Royal Melbourne Hospital. The first thing the doctors and surgeons asked me was: is there any family history of cancer in your family? You can imagine how upsetting it was to not only be told of this diagnosis but to then have to wonder whether I've inherited this from my paternal family.'

I thought about what might have happened on that fateful day if Rel hadn't already been aware she was donor conceived. Would her parents have told her the truth, amid the emotional maelstrom of finding out she had a terminal illness? Or would they have said nothing and let her continue to tell the specialists her social dad's medical history? I was glad that her parents hadn't faced that impossible choice, and at least Rel hadn't had to go through further upheaval when she was already suffering so much.

'I have never been ill in my life. There is no history of cancer on my maternal side of the family and there were no real warning signs that this illness would strike at such a young age. It is believed that a person who is diagnosed with stage-four – medically deemed to be "incurable" – bowel cancer has likely inherited it through their genes. When I was first told about this diagnosis by my surgeons following emergency surgery to remove the large tumour, which had caused my large bowel to rupture, he said it was most likely related to a genetic factor. At this point I cried, not only for the fact that I was now terminally ill, but also as I most likely inherited this disease from my paternal family and my anonymous sperm donor, T5.

'Never having a complete medical history was never a concern to me, until this year. And now I see why it is vital that not only donor-conceived people have access to their genetic information, but they are also given full access to their medical histories and where possible this is updated every five years or so. The most frustrating thing in all of this is the system that has helped to create me is destroying me by leaving me powerless to know basic information regarding my identity and, more importantly, my own health. If I had this knowledge upon finding out at fifteen years of age I would have been able to make the decision to be tested for this type of cancer. The choice to be tested would have been mine. The cancer may also not have grown by this point, or at least not be metastasised, having spread extensively to my liver and lungs, deeming me incurable. Maybe it could have been caught early, giving me the opportunity to beat it, but as it stands the prognosis is grim. My oncologist told me that on average people who present as I do can expect to live for approximately five years *at most*. I am not ready to die and have started chemotherapy, but this is to increase my life expectancy and it is a terrible experience to have to go through. I cannot work or enjoy the life that I once knew. I feel like my youth has been taken away from me and I am furious to think that this could have been prevented. I cannot explain what it's like to have to face such questions about mortality at the age of twenty-nine.'

The MPs in suits watched uncomfortably as Rel talked about her impending death. Jane Garrett's eyes were bright with tears. Despite the evidence, and Rel's own words, deep down I didn't really believe that she was going to die. She was so alive, retaining the vivacious qualities that made such an impression on me the first time we met.

'I am also concerned that my eight half-siblings who were conceived by the same donor, T5, may be walking about and carrying this possible disease without knowing it. Not only might they have no idea that they are donor conceived, they may also be terminally ill. They may have passed this illness on to any children they have. This diagnosis does not only affect me, it possibly affects so many other people. And they should be made aware if this is the case. The effects of donor conception are intergenerational.

'In seeking to access my records and information about my biological father, sperm donor T5, I am not wishing to impede on his privacy or cause him any undue effects. What I want is something that most people take for granted: the choice to know their ancestry, their identity and their complete medical history. I never realised how great an impediment answering "unknown" to the question of paternal medical history on my medical forms would be. Having to know my genetic history for health reasons was truly one of the last reasons I ever felt the urge to find my donor, and now it's probably the most important thing.

'So it's really important to me now that I can know who my paternal family is. I would like to meet them or know of them before I die. I want to be able to say that I truly know myself before

I die. I do not want to leave this earth without this knowledge. But the reality is I am facing dying before I know who my father is, who my paternal family is, who I am.'

Rel's cheeks were slightly pink. She had been talking in an even tone of voice, but now she slowed her speech and spoke louder, like she was trying to be heard by someone hard of hearing.

'I am beyond angry. I am beyond frustrated. And I am tired of waiting for the legislation to change so that *all* donor-conceived people are treated with the dignity and respect that every other Victorian is awarded – that they are provided with *their truth*.'

Physically she was fragile, but her brown eyes flashed; her courage remained formidable as she spoke.

'Broadly speaking, I feel that the practice of donor conception has always been too far ahead of any ethical consideration given to the human implications of this medical treatment. I view donor conception primarily as a money-making industry that is mainly focused on enabling adults to have children at a price. I do not feel that the doctors have any true vested interests in the emotional or social consequences of what they do. In my experience with them, I feel especially strongly that the doctors who began this practice in the late 1970s here in Melbourne did so with their own interests at heart. They were eager to make history and went ahead and did so without properly considering what that meant to people like myself who they were helping to create.'

She summarised the reasons she was here again, and ended with a plea. 'I urge the state government to implement legislation awarding all donor-conceived people the same rights as every other Victorian – the right to know themselves and their kin.'

'Thank you for testifying here today and we are most impressed with your courage and wish you absolutely all the best,' said Jane.

'Thank you,' said Rel. 'I would like to thank you for your time today.'

Rel folded her speech, got up from the table and sat down next to me again. After spending half her life searching, explaining, advocating and begging, she looked very tired.

Six months after the public hearings, the Law Reform Committee completed their work on their inquiry, 'Access by Donor-Conceived People to Information about Donors'. TangledWebs and supporters sat in the public gallery to watch Law Reform Committee Member Donna Petrovich table the final report to parliament. She spoke about how the five committee members had held one view when they first began the inquiry, but reached consensus on a different view by its conclusion. None of us knew what influence our public submissions and testimony had had on the five members, or their paradigm shift, until we got our hands on a copy of the report.

When it finally arrived, I eagerly read the contents.

Recommendation 1: The Victorian Government introduce legislation to allow all donor-conceived people to obtain identifying information about their donors.

Helen's advice about 'the power of the individual experience' had proved true. Our stories – particularly Rel's – were powerful, and the committee had listened.

We celebrated on the steps of Parliament House, clutching copies of the report like talismans. The political debate had come such a long way, but we were under no illusions. There was still a long way to go to turn these non-binding recommendations into law.

When I read the report in detail I was struck by how the cloak of donor anonymity had created the conditions for ethical breaches to flourish. Despite programs operating out of public hospitals, they had absolutely no accountability or transparency. A submission from Kate Dobby, whom I had spoken to in the past and who was was intimately familiar with the donor records, reported,

> Some Clinics, Hospitals and Doctors may oppose the granting of equal rights to access information for the donor conceived, not only because it exposes the weaknesses and inadequacies of past records, but because of what is revealed about past practices. Egg swapping, sperm mixing, donors' identities not being verified or donors being encouraged to donate under pseudonyms, offering free vasectomies and sperm storage, STD testing and [university] course credits in exchange for donating, knowingly creating up to thirty separate families or an excess of forty children from one donor, using anonymous donors imported from interstate without paperwork, recoding donors, the practice of on-donation, utilising patients as donors whilst they are still in [infertility] treatment and using donors for whom valid consent could not be verified are just some of the practices that I know to have occurred in Victoria.

The dark shadow over that bright March day was news of Rel's worsening health. Chemotherapy had trimmed the vines of the cancer that grew within her body but as the drugs lost their potency the root remained strong. In response Rel embarked on a strict plant-based diet of unprocessed foods, and tried reiki and various therapies, but the tumours grew back with renewed vigour.

Six months after the Law Reform Committee tabled their final report, a group of us went out to lunch at a café in North Melbourne to celebrate Rel's thirtieth birthday. Myf had baked a lovely vegan chocolate cake as a present. It was early September and the plum trees lining the streets of Melbourne were exploding with fragrant pink and white blossoms, but after a year and a half of cancer and chemotherapy Rel looked awfully thin and frail. She had cut off her dreadlocks and wore her wavy brown hair in a fringed bob.

The conversation turned to Rel's search. Under the shadow cast by her diagnosis, the search for T5 had become more urgent. We talked about how the law reform process was taking too long and what other avenues might be available. With a pained look in her warm brown eyes Rel confided to us in a whisper, 'Maybe T5 doesn't want to be found. I've come to a place of acceptance that I'll never meet him.'

My throat felt tight.

That evening I raged to Gerry about the injustice. 'It isn't fair. After all Rel's courage and tenacity in telling her story, which was what convinced the bloody politicians to act, change is going to come too fucking late to help her!'

A couple of months after her thirtieth birthday, I heard from Myf that Rel had been linked up with palliative-care services. It was a race against time. What else could be done? We brought her plight to the attention of several politicians within the Victorian parliament, including the Law Reform Committee chair, Clem Newton-Brown.

*Clemency ~ *

A power given to public officials to grant leniency or mercy, to lower the harshness of a punishment.

Rel had been searching for T5 for half her life. She deserved some clemency. But what had been her crime?

After her tremendous fifteen-year struggle, finally there was a breakthrough. Clem referred her case up the chain and in February then premier, Ted Baillieu, cut through the legal stasis and authorised the release of Rel's records from the Public Record Office to the Attorney-General's Office so they could at long last write to her donor.

'It was like this psychic switch went off in my heart, my mind, my soul. I hadn't seen her for thirty years; I wasn't even aware of her, and suddenly she's there. I just love her so much.'

These words were how Raymondo Tonna, aka T5, described first meeting Rel at his home near Ballarat in regional Victoria. As Helen had alluded to Rel all those years ago he was indeed of Maltese heritage. They had the same passionate, warm brown eyes that lit up in mutual delight when they saw one another. In meeting Ray, Rel discovered they both wrote and performed poetry and music. Ray exuded a love that I hoped might allow Rel's wounded heart to heal.

Shortly after their meeting, Rel was hospitalised. Ray took the train almost every day to Melbourne to spend time with her. She was stoic in her suffering. Even as she lay gravely ill she worried about the welfare of her eight half-siblings listed in the donor records. She wanted them to be screened for bowel cancer, but was powerless to pass on this development in their medical history.

In late March on the Tuesday before Easter, Myf phoned me at work to tell me Rel had died. Feelings of shock and numbness rose anew. We spoke about how Rel and Ray's time together was beautiful, yet so bittersweet for its brevity, for what might have been.

At her funeral I felt overwhelmed by the enormity of the loss. Rel had been such a guiding light and inspiration to me. I didn't know how to let her go. I glanced over at poor Ray who likewise was in a daze. The light in his brown eyes had gone dim and he looked heartbroken. He had found and lost a daughter in the space of six short weeks.

After the Catholic service Rel was buried under a flowering gumtree, close to water, beneath a white cross that simply stated her name.

I visited Ray and his partner, Susie, a few times. Ray enjoyed spending time with people who had known Rel and who could tell stories that captured her essence. On one visit we watched the DVD of a student documentary Rel's best friend, Danielle, had shot in 2005 about Rel's search for T5. As Rel had told the Law Reform Committee, when her parents first told her the truth the feisty fifteen-year-old went to see Professor Kovacs, her mother's treating doctor, to ask if he could help her find T5. The film we watched captured the moment when, as a young woman in her early twenties, Rel returned to Professor Kovacs's office to again ask for his help.

Likening it to my experience meeting the governor, I was intrigued to watch another renegade miracle baby return to confront their maker. Danielle's footage captured the power imbalance, the height and age difference between Rel and Professor Kovacs. He wears a suit and tie with a lanyard around his neck. In the background his bookshelves are filled with textbooks and the wall is crowded with framed certificates and his Member of the Order of Australia. Ray, Susie and I watched Rel on the screen sit opposite Professor Kovacs and say to him, 'Just looking at the Infertility Treatment Act, it doesn't stipulate anywhere in there that you can't try to contact my donor on my behalf more than once.'

Kovacs replied, 'There's no legal – there's no legal specification. It's purely an ethical and moral one.'

'Yep,' said Rel, nodding vigorously. Watching the footage I was acutely aware how easily that could have been me being stonewalled.

Professor Kovacs continued. 'I had the ability to go down, find the records, find the latest known address of the donor. The problem was that we asked for some help from the board of the institute, the Prince Henry's Institute where we worked. And the recommendation they gave was that we could try and contact the donor only once and not harass them, because it's possible that some of these donors hadn't told their families that they had donated. It was a fairly unusual name and when I went to the phone book there were only about three or four of those names in the White Pages, so in fact I wrote to all of those addresses saying, "If you're the gentleman who was involved with the project at Prince Henry's in the 1970s or 1980s – whatever it was – could you please contact me?" But I got no response.'

Ray was outraged. 'I never received any letter from Dr Kovacs. I was always listed in the phone book; up to date on the electoral roll, Medicare – everything. Why didn't he find me? If any doctor had phoned me and said, "By the way, you know, you've got a child out there somewhere," I would have moved heaven and hell to get to her.'

I couldn't accept that all Rel's anger, bitterness and frustration had just been a terrible misunderstanding predicated on a letter sent by Professor Kovacs but never received by Ray. A Shakespearean tragedy, like Friar Lawrence's note never received by Romeo in Mantua. But that was fiction and this was real life. I thought about Ian, the donor who had received a letter from Monash IVF about his seven donor-conceived offspring. In that case the letter had been forwarded through multiple addresses to reach him. What circumstance of chance meant that Ray had never received the letter from Dr Kovacs?

'Rel was a bit suspicious because she never saw a copy of any letter, or knew for sure it had even been sent,' I explained to Ray and Susie. 'She always believed Dr Kovacs could have been more generous with his attempts to contact T5, rather than just trying once. She used to describe herself as a "Thing", and Kovacs as her Dr Frankenstein, as her nemesis in this battle to try to discover the identity of T5. She never felt like he empathised with her situation, and that his actions showed his main priority was protecting the privacy of the donors. I remember once Rel showed me a letter from Kovacs in which he wrote, "Whilst I understand you might be a bit frustrated; the situation was made quite clear to your mum and dad before they commenced the treatment." She was indignant. She said to me, "So I'm just going to have to deal with that, obviously. That's his stance on it."'

Ray was similarly upset. 'Maybe all that hurt, all that frustration, manifested as a physical scar, that cancer. I mean, *hello*, what about the mind-body connection?' he said, gesticulating wildly, as Rel used to do, between his heart and head.

It didn't bear thinking about.

It was heartbreaking to know that the fifteen years Rel had spent in fruitless searching had been unnecessary, that her anguish could have been avoided if someone had been empowered to ask a simple question.

I smiled sadly. 'I'm so glad you found each other, and Rel got to meet you before she died. Rel taught me a great life lesson.'

'What's that?' asked Ray.

'Never give up.'

Thirteen

After Rel died the slow gears of government ground on. To tell the full story of all the trials and tribulations of lobbying to enact the Law Reform Committee's recommendations would require another book. As part of this process the Victorian government ordered a special consultation with past donors in which about half said they were supportive of the proposed law change, and three-quarters said they were personally supportive of contact with their offspring. A number of donors were firmly opposed to the proposed removal of anonymity.

One of these was Ben. He started doing a little bit of media and was quoted describing the proposed law change as a broken promise. He also added his details to the VARTA-run Voluntary Register, the conduit to share information or make contact with his other donor-conceived children.

I understood that my mother, Ben and I stood on different sides of the donor-conception triangle and each held a valid but disparate perspective based on our own experiences. I also understood why some donors believed it was wrong for the government to go back on the promise of anonymity given to them by the clinics. I firmly agreed that donors had the right to privacy and any contact had to be mutually wanted, just as it is in any other type of relationship. But the promise given by the original doctors was premised on an unethical framework that discounted the impact on the most vulnerable party – the children that were created. Rel had borne the consequences of such a system. It seemed untenable to continue in this way.

A further consideration was the powerful combination of emerging technologies and social media, which was rapidly making donor anonymity an obsolete concept. The exponentially growing popularity of consumer-DNA-testing databases meant donors could now be found anyway, even if they hadn't personally tested.

Nevertheless, I faced a new and alarming calculus. Here we were on the brink of convincing the government to enact legislation honouring Rel's life – but lobbying publicly in support of it might threaten the relationship with Ben I'd worked so hard to establish. I didn't know what to do except cordon off the proposed law change as another taboo topic, to avoid the tension. Just one more blank space, something better left unsaid.

For my thirtieth birthday I held a picnic in the Botanic Gardens that my half-sister Charlotte attended. She gave me a lovely necklace as a present, along with the business card of her next-door neighbour. Belinda Hawkins was a writer, journalist and producer of human-interest documentaries for the ABC's *Australian Story*. I gave her a call. We discussed her vision of telling my story in a way that would personalise the abstract issues of donor conception.

In speaking out publicly about my experiences I wanted to illuminate a little of the history of donor conception in Australia.

I could see the potential for television to impact the opinion of hundreds of thousands of viewers and publicise the need for the law to change. It was also an opportunity to challenge the preconceptions (pun intended) about people born from assisted reproductive treatment: that we are perpetual babies, that if we are loved and wanted enough then nothing else matters, and on it goes. On the other hand, in my experience doing media was fraught with twin dangers: exposure to hurtful trolls, who ironically hid behind their own anonymity; and the steep cost of damage to family relationships.

I procrastinated for a month in anticipatory dread, before I finally started calling members of my family to float the proposal and find out their reaction to the idea of my involvement with *Australian Story*. Initially these conversations didn't go well and everything was on indefinite hold. Six months later there was a shift. Still, I remained nervous about approaching other key people to ask if they were willing to be interviewed on camera. I was sure nobody was particularly keen, especially in light of what Ben thought about the legal situation.

My mum told me doing the show was a bad idea, but agreed to participate for me. It was her language of love. Eventually, during another visit to the coast, I found the opportunity to ask Ben. His personal preference was to remain out of the limelight, but to my absolute surprise he said yes to being involved.

Filming took a long time, almost a year. Belinda bunkered down with the editor to produce the final cut on a two-part episode featuring me, a donor-conceived journalist called Sarah Dingle and, posthumously, Rel.

As I counted down the days until the piece would air, I tackled something that felt extremely awkward – telling Dad that I knew I was donor conceived and had met Ben. We just didn't have the sort of relationship to discuss these things in person, so I composed an email.

I wrote,

> I want to reassure you that finding out I am donor conceived and meeting the donor has not changed my feelings towards you in any way. You are still my dad. I think it is human nature to have curiosity and I hope you can understand why I felt I had to find out more information. I really hope it doesn't hurt your feelings or arouse any insecurity that I have conducted this search and met these people. It has nothing to do with anything you did or didn't do and I am grateful that I had a good upbringing. I really appreciate all the things you did for me and all your involvement in athletics training, and flying lessons etc. I really want to emphasise that you are still my dad.

He seemed to take it okay. He didn't ask questions or refer directly to what I had written, but later made a passing reference that if my 'friends' were ever on the Sunshine Coast they would be welcome to stop by for lunch.

Consciously or subconsciously, Gerry and I booked a three-week holiday to Canada and the US that coincided with the airing of the *Australian Story* episode, which Belinda titled 'Searching for C11'. I hoped by the time we returned it would all be over.

While overseas I received an email from Helen.

> Dear Lauren,
>
> Well done with the program. It was terrific. No one could possibly think it wasn't reasonable for people who are donor conceived to seek contact with their donors, and would see that the

world does not collapse around them or their families if they do.

Hopefully good stuff comes from airing the issues, and the people themselves. I was so proud of Narelle and her family. As well as you and yours of course.

All the very best for the future,

Well done,

Helen

It was good to hear from her. Any rift we had was water under the bridge. I was grateful for all her work and support.

Returning to Australia, I finally watched the *Australian Story* documentary. I thought Belinda did a great job presenting the human drama within the story. Then I made the mistake of reading the comments on an opinion piece I had written for the ABC's online forum *The Drum*. They contained all the usual tropes: poor donors needed protecting from us ratbag donor-conceived kids who wanted to invade their lives, steal their money and inherit their property. I was labelled self-centred and selfish because they assumed my advocacy work was going to lead to fewer people signing up to be donors. Others posted slightly sinister comments saying that if I wasn't happy with the agreements that were entered into I could choose to abort myself as an adult.

After a lot of positive feedback from friends and acquaintances about the show, I felt a bit stunned at these responses from the general public. Intellectually, I knew that the internet was the perfect forum for trolls, but the words still hurt. Although I hoped these comments weren't representative, they made me worry that most people had no concept of what it feels like to be donor conceived, and even Rel's story wasn't enough to trigger sympathy. Eventually, I learnt it is a much better idea never to read the comments, but they did illustrate to me how some people think about the issues, and the need for an alternative narrative to change the story, increase awareness and help sway public opinion.

On a much more positive note, Belinda's dogged hard work as producer was rewarded with a Walkley Award in the category of social equity journalism.

The documentary touched many people's lives with myriad ripple effects. At their street Christmas party, a neighbour told my mother that she had never revealed to her family that she was adopted. However, after watching *Australian Story* and seeing how Mum had the courage to tell me the truth, she had been inspired to open up to her own children.

A month after the program aired, I was on a work trip to Brisbane and popped down to buy some breakfast from a nearby 7-Eleven. As I perused the cereals I was stunned to be recognised by a man about my age who had seen the show. In a halting voice he told me he was also donor conceived. In our short exchange I got his details and promised to send him the link to the RUDC (R U Donor Conceived?) Facebook page. He subsequently joined, and we kept in touch. I remembered how lonely and isolated I had felt when I first learnt I was donor conceived and was delighted at this connection.

Membership of the RUDC Facebook page steadily rose. In fascination, I read some beautifully expressed posts. One young woman wrote:

> We're all here searching for answers, for closure, for new beginnings, for love and acceptance, for our experiences and feelings to be validated and to be welcomed into a close circle of unusual circumstances that only we would ever understand.

> Whether you were told willingly from very young, or found out accidentally in your 30s+, you are loved, we're all here for each other and regardless of if we are related or not, different religions, cultures, nationalities or upbringings, we here in RUDC have a very special love and connection to one-another that no-one else could understand. They may sympathise or empathise with all the best intentions, but never truly understand. That's what makes us all in this group connected, special and unique.

Another post began,

> Disenfranchised grief. Yeah, a heavy topic for a Saturday morning! How do you resolve or heal from the loss and pain from something that you innately yearned for but never had? I find it challenging that those around you may not believe you have the need, or right, to grieve for a relationship that never existed. And while finding out (at 38!) that I am DC has opened a whole new potential world, it has also opened a whole new world of loss … loss of time, family and discovery of long-held secrets. I feel grief for the loss of relationships that could have been and links that may never eventuate. With five unknown siblings out there, the reality is we may never connect unless they conduct DNA tests or parents tell them of their DC status – that hurts. Another loss or perhaps another opportunity for hope.

After a sustained lobbying effort from TangledWebs and supporters, the Victorian Labor Party – in opposition at the time – announced an election promise to implement the full recommendations of the Law Reform Committee's report. Labor went on to win the state election and the final step to achieving legislative change was holding them accountable to implement their election promise.

Within the walls of parliament the case for change was prosecuted by a tri-partisan group: the deputy chair of the Law Reform Committee, Jane Garrett, and member Anthony Carbines – better known as 'Carby' – worked tirelessly as key proponents of law reform within the Labor Party. The new health minister, Jill Hennessy, was a shining light in sponsoring the bill. Clem Newton-Brown, chair of the Law Reform Committee, was the key ally in the Liberal Party, and Sue Pennicuik from the Greens provided continuous support. They were all hardworking representatives who really did care about their constituents. Working side by side with these MPs exposed me to a different side of politics beyond the cynicism so commonly seen in the media.

Once more I did the mental calculus, counting up my wins and losses, and this time I decided to withdraw from participating in any more frontline media. A multitude of other donor-conceived people made the difficult decision to step up and tell their stories. Various people were interviewed on television for *Lateline*, appeared in print in *Women's Weekly*, or spoke on radio on Jon Faine's *Mornings* program. Others developed podcasts, spoke at public forums, undertook PhDs, and much, much more. They were all gorgeously eloquent and it was among my proudest moments to realise I could step back because RUDC, which had sprung up out of the work begun by TangledWebs that built upon the work of the Donor Conception Support Group, was now a self-sustaining movement.

In June 2015, with sponsorship from the William Buckland Foundation, we put on an RUDC conference in which a record fifty donor-conceived people from around Australia and New Zealand gathered in Melbourne to share information, and organise and provide peer support. The keynote speaker was Chief Justice of the Family Court of Australia John Pascoe. I met dozens of donor-conceived people, some of whom became very dear to me.

Over time, assisted by the internet and regular in-person meetings, we formed an entire community and I had the privilege to hear the personal stories of many donor-conceived people from all around Australia. In this context, I realised that what David de Kretser did for me was truly an exceptional outcome. The majority of donor-conceived people conceived via clinics had terrible experiences. A woman from Queensland contacted her clinic over and over for nineteen years and was told first that her records had been lost in a fire, then lost in a flood, then intentionally destroyed. She finally met with her mother's treating doctor and discovered this was all lies, as he explained to her the records were 'out the back' all along. Another person conceived at the same clinic was told there were never any records, and furthermore that because she wasn't their patient she should never contact the clinic again.

This pattern wasn't limited to Australia. Another woman from our RUDC Facebook forum who was conceived in New Zealand wrote to her mother's treating doctor. He replied that he couldn't tell her anything because of anonymity. She contacted him yearly and was variously told there were no records or records had been destroyed. Eventually, he released the donor's non-identifying information to her, and a few years later told her there had been five other pregnancies. The doctor said he couldn't find the donor on the national medical system, and suggested that her donor was either deceased or living overseas. Eventually, she met another donor-conceived person from the same clinic who had the same donor code. A DNA test confirmed they were half-siblings. They realised they had both been in touch with the same doctor over the years asking for information, but he had never mentioned a sibling or put them in touch with each other. After fourteen years the doctor finally agreed to search again for her donor, not as a result of her persistent requests, but because her parents wrote to him and asked him to. She got a call from the doctor saying he had found her donor, but he had died the previous year, too late for her to ever ask questions or meet him in person. The next year she did her own investigations through DNA testing and finally found out her biological father's name. She was shocked and angry to discover he had never moved from the suburb he was living in when he first donated sperm. You can see why many donor-conceived people are sceptical about their clinic being forthcoming with the truth.

On the RUDC Facebook forum people shared their stories of the ongoing real-life impacts stemming from questionable practices that occurred within donor clinics under the cloak of anonymity. With the permission of those affected, I have included a few examples of the enormity of these ethical breaches, that go far beyond record destruction.

Prior to Victoria's legislation enacted in 1988 that created the Central Register, clinics didn't require donors to provide an identity document to prove their name and age. The doctors found it acceptable to inseminate their female patients with sperm of unknown provenance, which doesn't seem particularly respectful of women's health. Belatedly, some protocols were established after four women contracted HIV from donor insemination in the 1980s (all of these women later died from AIDS, including one who left behind a motherless child who fortunately did not contract the virus). A donor-conceived friend of mine reported that after contacting her donor they had a one-off meeting during which he told her he had donated sperm to a Victorian clinic as a sixteen-year-old boy on school holidays, for the cash payment. She was born when he was just seventeen. That clinics accepted children as sperm donors was shocking enough, but there was a further terrible twist. Almost a decade later this same woman matched with a biological uncle on the Ancestry DNA database, only to find he was unrelated to the man she had been told was her donor. To her shock she discovered the clinic had deliberately or negligently written the wrong donor code in her mother's file. Outrageously, even though she now knows through DNA testing who her true biological father is, there is no official confirmation because the incorrect donor code written in the records is deemed by legislation as the 'truth'. Thus, she is not permitted access to the non-identifying information that should be her right to know, such as how many donor-conceived half-siblings she has.

Another donor-conceived friend found herself at the centre of another incredibly messy situation. Through DNA testing she matched with half-siblings from South Australia who had a completely different donor code from her clinic in Victoria. Eventually, an investigation revealed that her biological father had donated sperm to various clinics under multiple names and donor codes, even at one point impersonating a dead man. This man was a frequent donor and the clinic shipped some of his sperm from Victoria to South Australia without tracing paperwork, where it was recoded to create yet another donor code. The paper trail is incomplete, but through just two of his multiple donor codes she has thirty-one half-siblings. There are likely to be more. This could be determined by DNA testing, but the donor-conceived woman learnt her donor has such a serious mental health condition that he was deemed incapable of giving informed consent. Thus, she finds herself in the unenviable situation of being unable to even confirm how many half-siblings she has, let alone achieve her original aim of passing on important hereditary health information to them.

Sarah Dingle, the donor-conceived journalist who appeared with me and Rel on *Australian Story*, meticulously documented the appalling ethical failings and cover-ups of the assisted reproductive treatment industry in her book, *Brave New Humans*. Interweaving her own experience dealing with the Royal North Shore Hospital with the broader story, she showed that practices such as deliberate destruction of medical records weren't limited to one or two rogue doctors. It was systematic.

Apart from work by a handful of donor-conceived people like Sarah, and some references within the Victorian Law Reform Committee's inquiry, there has been surprisingly little documentation of the ethical breaches that occurred under the cloak of donor anonymity. My hope is one day we can progress to a proper independent inquiry that perhaps might even result in a national apology, as given by then Prime Minister Julia Gillard in 2013 to people hurt by past adoption policies and practices.

Some people on the RUDC forum – mostly those conceived outside the clinic system – have had much more positive experiences of their family formation. A donor-conceived woman explains,

> I have had a fairly unique situation compared to many people in this group. I have a known donor, a gay man and a friend of my parents, and grew up having a relationship much like with an uncle with him and my half-siblings (he donated to two single women and a lesbian couple too). I've had a really positive experience and my siblings and I are so proud of who we are and how we got here.

Within our community everyone has a different story, spanning hurt and struggle to philosophical acceptance or wholehearted pride in their conception story. Wherever donor-conceived people sit on this spectrum there exists a kernel of shared understanding. We have a way of being together with a sense of knowing, without having to explain, that bonds us like veteran soldiers from the same regiment. Rel's dream of a donor-conceived army had come true. Our theatre of battle was the Victorian parliament.

I donned my warm clothing – woollen thermals, a polar fleece and gloves – to prepare for the uncharted journey over the Wind River Range. Gerry was more casual, wearing a merino thermal top and his characteristic shorts.

Venturing past the end of the marked trail we came to a riot of wildflowers: clumps of buttery yellow daisies and scarlet Indian paintbrush fringed by curls of bright green spongy moss. Further ahead to my left a scoured, grey glacier hung above a colossal snowfield. There was beauty in the music made by the white, foaming creek fed by its melt. We were in a curved basin, its cliff faces stained by the black shadows of past waterfalls. As we climbed, our bodies formed two small dots reflected in the upper lake near our camp site, though there was nobody around to see.

The incline steepened and the narrowing grassy valley became choked with boulders. As the ground disappeared and the horizon shrank I made my way by rock hopping. In the absence of a trail we navigated the jumbled mass of rocks by following the waterline. Miniature gardens of succulents and orange and green lichen peeked out of sheltered niches, like terrariums. These tiny signposts helped us follow the drainage and keep our bearings on the distant pass, a narrow notch between the mountains, lost within countless shapes of grey and white.

Up and up we hiked. Eventually, the boulder field disappeared beneath the snowfield, curiously tinted with splotches of red.

'Whoops, forgot to pack the crampons,' I called out to Gerry, half in jest, half in concern. We didn't have any traction devices, ice axes or even hiking poles.

'I guess we'll have to try some old-fashioned stone-age mountaineering,' said Gerry, picking up an axe-shaped rock.

As we began our ascent of the snowfield sweat formed on my stomach, back, armpits and forehead. Out of breath with climbing, I stopped to rest, closing my eyes and listening to the soft gurgle of water trickling beneath my feet. I hoped the icy crust of snow-pack wouldn't collapse under my weight. My shirt under my backpack was stained with sweat but, standing still, I quickly cooled and began to shiver. Opening my eyes I saw Gerry, incongruous in his shorts as he stood in the middle of the colossal field of white. Six months into our trip his curly hair and beard had grown wild.

The snowfield steepened almost imperceptibly with every step and I began to hike more slowly to economise effort. My cadence dropped, my breath deepened in the thin air, and I felt my increased heart rate pulsing in my palms. On the next step up I slid backwards, so I started following Gerry, who used the axe-shaped rock to hack steps into the ever-steepening snow. Straightening up, I turned around to stare down the slope. It was exciting how high and exposed we were. There was a thrilling and seductive aspect to the danger. The present pulsated, like my heart pumping hard in my chest.

As we finally reached the end of the snowfield I stepped onto the ash-grey scree field that lay beyond, thinking the worst was behind us. But the gravelly pebbles shifted under my weight and immediately I began to slide again. 'It's steep!' I cried out, crouching low to lean in against the slope, the weight of my backpack threatening to buck me off the mountain. Resuming the climb, each step created a miniature landslide that skidded to a precarious halt. Two steps forward, one step back.

Ahead of me Gerry backslid and dislodged a larger rock. 'Watch out!' he called as it gathered momentum and clattered past me.

Twisting around, I watched it tumble down the snowfield into the void of space below. Uselessly, my mind estimated how far I might slide if I slipped. One hundred metres? Five hundred? The flat perspective of snow made it hard to judge distance. Uncertainty can fill any space. Turning back, I inhaled and exhaled the cold alpine air to get a grip. Once again the horizon shrank as my eyes cast down and scanned the shale for minuscule ledges, seeking any hint of relief from the appalling gradient. Every fibre of my being focused on the task of placing one foot in front of the other, kicking toeholds to maintain my tenuous grip and avoid falling into the abyss below. The world shrank to a breath, followed by a step, a pause, and another breath. Eventually exhaustion limited my energy for thought and I became nothing. Body, self, space and time all vanished. It wasn't a philosopher but a physicist – Albert Einstein – who remarked that the only real time lies within us. I was in this high-altitude landscape and the landscape was within me.

Almost imperceptibly, the slope began to level out towards the pass. A burst of summit fever pushed me up and over the last tough boulder scramble to the short saddle that sat between two peaks. A few steps later an incredible vista opened up into the next valley and the surrounding massifs. Feeling a strange mixture of exhaustion and exhilaration from the overwhelming splendour of standing eye to eye with the saw-toothed crests in every direction I turned and hugged Gerry,

'We made it!'

I was suddenly overcome by tears sparked by a mixture of relief at being able to rest and a glorious sense of leaving my comfort zone behind to embrace something entirely unknown. Brushing the tears away, I pointed wordlessly towards a small creek fed by a mighty glacier that clung to the near vertical peak enclosing the newly visible valley. The contours of the landscape slowly flattened into an inviting meadow cut by the stream that meandered through the rockfall-strewn valley floor over a thousand metres below. Like my excursion to the mesa top, once again I stared down upon the Green River.

Sweat cooling, I put on my puffy jacket and sat down on a boulder. Mesmerised by the staggering beauty, I felt a temptation to remain. But in the ringing silence of almost four thousand metres of elevation – the absence of birdsong or buzz of insects – I perceived a warning that we two pilgrims had strayed into inhuman heights where we didn't belong.

Gerry stared down at the stream below us and frowned. 'We better go,' he said. 'I don't think this is a place for us to linger.'

Fourteen

Nearly three years after Rel's death a bill finally arrived before the Victorian parliament to enact the full recommendations of the Law Reform Committee's report. Colloquially we called it Narelle's Law.

The bill followed the model suggested by Professor Sonia Allan. Although not all records of donor-treatment procedures were still intact, where records existed, donor-conceived people would get retrospective access to identifying information about their donor, with donors given legal rights to control the level of contact they were comfortable with, all the way up to a 'no contact' veto. On the final sitting day of the year the bill, backed by the new Labor government, passed the lower house and parliament rose for the summer break. In two months, when parliament recommenced, the upper house would vote on the bill. If the bill passed it would become a world-first law.

That summer was the critical moment, the culmination of a decade and a half of lobbying by TangledWebs and organisations such as VANISH and the Donor Conception Support Group. There was no guarantee the bill would succeed; it was controversial and openly opposed by the assisted reproductive treatment industry, some donors, individual doctors and powerful lobby groups such as the Australian Medical Association. I knew that political machinations and posturing were taking place behind the scenes that summer and I should be out there, *agitating*. But I couldn't. I had nothing left.

For years I had drawn on a seemingly bottomless well of energy that at its heart was generated from rage against my own powerlessness. Countless hours of advocacy, media and lobbying had threatened my closest relationships with the family I grew up with, as well as the new connections I'd worked so hard to establish. Now, I felt overcome by a tremendous *Weltschmerz*. I was completely depleted; it was impossible to draw water from an empty well. And so, with a strange feeling of equanimity, I slipped through the summer without writing a single letter or making a single phone call.

After the summer break, on a Tuesday afternoon in late February, TangledWebs and supporters, including Rel's sister Michelle, made the well-trodden journey into Parliament House and crowded into the public gallery overlooking the Legislative Council chamber. We left an empty seat in honour of Rel as the upper house commenced debate on the bill.

Unlike the lower house, in the upper house the Labor government did not have a majority. We knew Labor and the Greens were supportive, which totalled nineteen votes, but the bill required twenty-one votes to pass and become law. The Liberal Party had been given a free vote, but in general the legislation was too radical for the conservative MPs to support. Our best hope lay in convincing two of the five cross-benchers to vote yes.

As we slipped into Parliament House and took our seats I didn't know what the outcome was going to be, but I knew it was going to be close. In my nervousness I kept up a steady stream of text messages with an advisor to the health minister (who was sponsoring the bill), trying to figure out what the hell was going on with the vote. Did we have the numbers? Or were we going to fail at the last hurdle?

One of the cross-benchers, Dr Rachel Carling-Jenkins from the Democratic Labour Party, stood up first. 'I rise today to speak to the *Assisted Reproductive Treatment Amendment Bill 2015*. This bill has caused me to think very deeply, to weigh up all the different sides of the argument and to feel conflicted – deeply, deeply conflicted. I believe very strongly that every child has a right to know their biological history. I am a very strong advocate for correct birth certificates – that is, birth certificates which clearly state the biological mother and the biological father of a child. Genetic heritage is important to the fundamental and very human question of "Who am I?" This is why late last year I first read my *Adoption Amendment (Identifying Biological Parents) Bill 2015*. It is our right to know who we are.'

This sounds promising, I texted.

'Every child has a right to understand their genetic make-up and to know the details of their conception when this is possible. And so I do not oppose the intent of this bill, but I do take issue with some of the elements of the bill which appear to be unfair and harmful to donors and donor-conceived people alike.'

She went on to list some of the views from her constituents who had corresponded with her about the bill.

'As I said at the beginning of my contribution, this bill leaves me deeply conflicted. It is fraught with potential problems, and I look forward to examining these further through the committee process in order to gain further insight into the implications of this bill. I reserve my decision as to which way to vote on this bill until the committee stage is complete. However, based on some of the contributions that have already been made today, I am more inclined to vote against the bill at this stage.'

A sick feeling crept into my guts. Was decades of advocacy work about to be defeated at the last gasp? I cursed myself for not contacting Dr Carling-Jenkins over the summer break. Maybe I could have changed her mind, but it was too late. There was nothing I could do except sit and watch.

Next up was Bernie Finn from the Liberal Party. I remembered him from a previous meeting as a maverick character.

'Dr Carling-Jenkins said she is very deeply conflicted, and I have to say I am very deeply conflicted. There are very clear cases here for a yes vote, and there are very, very clear cases here for a no vote. What we have to do is balance up what carries more weight – what is more important to whom. I have to say that I am very grateful to my party, the Liberal Party, and to the leader, Matthew Guy, for agreeing very readily to a free vote on this bill.

'There is clearly, in debate on this bill, room for a discussion about the right to anonymity. I do not think there is any doubt about that. That is something that donors back prior to 1998 thought they had sewn up. They thought that was a promise – an ironclad promise. I have to say that I am not a big fan of retrospective legislation. I have never been a fan of retrospective legislation. Whatever the issue may be, it is something that I do not have a great deal of enthusiasm about supporting.'

Doesn't sound good. Sounds like he's landing in the same place as the DLP, I texted the advisor.

'What I would like to do is pay tribute to Clem Newton-

Brown, a former member for Prahran in the Legislative Assembly, who did a great deal of work in this area. He and I discussed this matter at length on a number of occasions.

'We all know that where we come from is very important to us. Some years ago even I went burrowing back to where I came from. I went back to an uncle who was a bishop in Ireland and who was in fact one of the founders of the Irish Republican Army, which is what we now know as the IRA, so I closed the book and I did not look at it again. I thought, "That was enough for anybody. I will give that a wide berth."'

I giggled.

'But it is nonetheless something that clearly is important to people and in this particular instance actually shapes their lives. It makes their lives different. It improves their lives if they can know what makes them do what they do, why they have blue eyes, why they have blond hair, why they walk with a limp and all of these sorts of things that are handed down through the years. It answers so many questions to know the genetic make-up of an individual. It answers the same questions for people to know who their parents are, who their grandparents are and so forth.

'I have to say that this is a red-letter day for this Parliament, because at this point in time I am actually going to support a bill on a matter such as this put forward by this government. Normally I would regard it as a stinking, rotten, foul government on these sorts of issues, but on this particular occasion I am actually going to support the government. Not only am I supporting the government but I am supporting the Greens.'

A fellow Liberal MP, Craig Ondarchie, interjected.

Bernie shouted in excitement, 'Somebody should get

Mr Ondarchie an ambulance! If anybody had any doubts about it being a red-letter day, that should settle it, because it is not very often that I agree with the Greens on much at all.'

Classic Bernie! 1 crucial swing vote, I texted as he sat down.

Next, Fiona Patten from the Sex Party stood up. Could she be the one to clinch the vote? My mouth was dry and there were butterflies in my stomach.

'I would like to add a small contribution to the debate on the *Assisted Reproductive Treatment Amendment Bill 2015*. As many members did, I received many really thoughtful personal emails and phone calls from people who were donor conceived during this time. I want to read one. It states, "I found out I was donor conceived this year in August after my mother tearfully confessed this to me. Not knowing and being lied to about who I am as a person has been hard but what has been even harder is that because of the current laws I may never know the whole truth. My experiences to date trying to find out my genetic and medical history have been frustrating and deeply hurtful. Yet I will keep searching, asking and begging for information because I need to know. I should not be denied information about who I am."'

I didn't know the person who had written this email, but was extremely impressed that only a few months after finding out the truth they had the strength to write to a member of parliament about their personal story. It had taken me years to get to that stage. I realised that I was strangely connected to this person who I knew nothing about because in the summer just past, when I had run out of energy to lobby for this bill, they had been there to pick up my slack. That was the power of building a movement – you didn't have to do it all alone.

I thought about this person's mother. She had probably lain

awake at night trying to figure out what the right thing to do was, just like my own mother had. The awful calculus. Two mothers, across a span of ten years, tearfully confessing the same secret. Maybe the parents of my three unknown donor-conceived half-siblings were similarly grappling with whether to reveal the difficult truth to their children. Maybe this bill would make a difference to their decision.

Fiona continued. 'One other woman who wrote to me was donor conceived prior to 1988 and she had had contact with her donor. She knew of a half-sister. That half-sister had a very rare form of a very aggressive breast cancer. She contacted the clinic where she had been donor conceived to pass on that information and to ask that clinic whether it would pass that information on to her other half-siblings. The clinic did not consider that that information was important at the time and refused to pass it on, so I think this bill will go a long way to assisting in those areas.'

This time I did know who Fiona was quoting. I turned to look at Myf, whose eyes were bright with tears. After Rel died, Myf had lost her half-sister to breast cancer, then been forced to endure the powerlessness of the clinics refusing to pass on the health history to her other half-siblings.

'We also understand that there is privacy and there is anonymity. This bill grants that those donors will lose that right to anonymity, but they do not lose the right to privacy, and I think we should separate the two.

'It is important that we understand that. Yes, I understand the retrospective nature, I understand the pain of the people who wrote to me who feel that we are breaching that anonymity that they felt they had when they felt they were doing the right thing. But we are not breaching their privacy, and I think that is where I was able to balance my decision in here.'

I mentally gave thanks for the genius of Professor Sonia Allan and her legal model that separated out information and privacy.

'This bill highlights the importance of clarity and support throughout the law-making process. It was unfair back in 1988, and this does rectify that for those people who were donor conceived. I fully acknowledge the fear and pain of some of the donors, who rightfully thought that their anonymity would be respected by law right to the very end. I am sorry that that is not so, but I do think, in weighing this up, the rights of those donor-conceived children outweigh that right to anonymity.'

After these speeches the MPs began shuffling across the chamber to the yes and no sides. Bernie the conservative and Fiona the progressive joined Labor and the Greens and we erupted in cheers from the public gallery as we realised we had the precious two votes. The parliamentary security guard tried to shush us – the public is supposed to bear silent witness – but we flagrantly ignored him and enjoyed the moment we had waited so long for. Disregarding another rule of parliament, I took a photo as evidence that the impossible had happened. By the agreed magic of the law, what was once painfully prohibited to me was now going to be accessible.

'What you don't know can't hurt you,' said the MP in my first advocacy meeting as he delivered a patronising pat on the shoulder. I knew he was wrong but I'd felt so powerless and weak. TangledWebs was just a small group of ordinary people busy with jobs, kids, study and the pressures of daily life who were committed to grassroots democracy. But by cultivating champions across parliament and banding together with politicians who supported us, we had shown our strength. We had stared down powerful lobby groups to create world-first legislative change. The achievement was testament to the capacity of personal stories to change hearts and minds.

After the vote we congregated in the Parliament House café accepting congratulations from a number of supportive MPs. I beamed, amid a glorious sensation of euphoria. Narelle's Law had passed.

Jane Garrett and Anthony Carbines both wore huge grins as they poured us all a glass of champagne. In the grinding hard work of being a member of parliament, here was a moment of satisfaction they were both clearly savouring.

'Thank you so much,' we chorused to Jane and Carby.

'Here's to you for making history!' said Jane. 'An unstoppable force.'

I recalled the life lesson I had learnt from Rel, to never give up. 'We're a bit like water on rock,' I grinned. 'We believe in erosion.'

We clinked glasses.

A year later, four years after Rel's death, her law was enacted, enabling all Victorian donor-conceived people to apply for information about their genetic heritage, regardless of when they were born. The gap I had fallen into was plugged by explicitly adding the orphaned Prince Henry's records to the Central Register, thus giving the ITA – now renamed VARTA – full guardianship over them.

Other members of the donor-conceived army went on to campaign in their own states, which in due course held their own inquiries that recommended changes mirroring Victoria's law reform. In a practical sense it hardly matters. Even in places without legislation, seismic changes are occurring as technology fast eclipses donor anonymity. Today, searches utilising consumer-DNA-testing databases, social media and public records often progress at light speed compared to the ponderous years of my own clumsy search. DNA testing has changed the game by inverting the power dynamic between clinical doctors and the individuals they helped create.

The Victorian legislation is no panacea and it doesn't always lead to the outcomes and answers people hope for. This journey offers no guarantees. After the law changed, Kim applied for information and her biological father placed a veto that barred all contact. However, she did receive his name and some form of resolution.

True to Rel's vision, the new law included provisions for serious medical information to be exchanged between donor siblings. The law also includes reciprocal rights for donor parents to request information about their offspring. As a result of these changes Ray was able to contact another of his donor-conceived daughters. Rel always longed to meet her half-siblings so I really wish they'd had a chance to meet. I think they would have got along great.

Like Rel and Ray, she is also an artist.

Continuing north-west the next day on our journey into the interior of the Wind River Range, we crested a ridge and then hiked down, down, down into a valley where the fir and spruce reappeared.

The deeper we hiked into the mountains, the less Gerry and I spoke. Instead, I listened to the wind in the trees and the chatter of squirrels. Grey, bushy tails darted here and there with sharp, springing movements. A hawk soared overhead on motionless wings. The fresh air carried a hint of pine sap and pollen.

Walking amid the forest, I stopped before a tree whose dark-green, fan-shaped branches arched elegantly towards the sky. Tracing the bark, my fingers read the message contained within its coarse stringy ridges. There was a certain regularity, a pattern, echoed in the arrangement of the forest. You might call it the grain of things. Branches, fern fronds and roots forked between higher and lower levels. The moss growing on tree roots was itself a miniature forest. Here, a different kind of circular economy was at play, deaf to the relentless drumbeat of human activity that had controlled me in my previous life. Balanced delicately, like raindrops on a twig, were partnerships between tall trees and tiny fungi, growth and sweet decay. I inhaled the subtle, clean smells of cycling chemistries, the scent of no waste. Respiration connected me with the trees, exchanging oxygen for carbon dioxide as the forest offered, freely, its gifts of coolness and shade. Weight of thought lifted, my mind felt lighter, soothed by the sense of things happening to a calendar paced by eternal transience and transient eternity.

Descending into the valley, I saw a bald eagle resting on a dead branch. It gazed down upon the pristine valley towards Squaretop Mountain, which rose like a citadel. Riffles of water circulated around boulders as the stream dropped over terraced rock platforms, exciting the river into the white roar of a waterfall topped by spray.

Just downstream of this waterfall the first of the log jams appeared. Broken sticks slashed at my legs, covering me in pine sap and grass seeds. Driftwood logs piled up at drunken angles, smashed like toothpicks by the current which rushed gleefully through the chaos it had created.

The stream quietened from roiling white water to a murmuring brook flanked by grassy banks. Around the next bend a lake appeared, luminous and pure. Its green waters reflected a lustre glimpsed in gemstones, bird of paradise feathers and ripe fruit; the colour from which creation springs.

After our long journey we set up camp beneath a tall spruce not far from the water's edge. Gerry and I fanned out to collect firewood. Pinecones made excellent fire starters and soon flames danced high from within a ring of rocks. The kettle atop the fire boiled and we carried our cups of tea down to the lake. In the late afternoon the wind extinguished into stillness, with no noise save for a boisterous duck and the staccato flight of bats.

The lake's water was utterly clear. And with clarity, suddenly I knew what question I needed to ask the accumulated wisdom that had flowed down the mountainsides and spilt over to become the Green River.

Who is my real *father? The one I grew up with or the one I share genes with?*

In reply, I saw into a unified image formed from transparency and reflection. Individual pebbles eroded from the mountaintops were clearly visible at the bottom of the lake. At the same time the water's surface reflected an image of the nearby snow-covered peaks. The lake's depths contained memories of my upbringing with Dad, stretching all the way back to earliest childhood, and its surface reflected traits I'd seen mirrored in Ben. In this way the lake revealed to me the distinction and unity between my dad who raised me and the man who provided half of my DNA. The pebbles and peaks were both part of the same mountain.

I undressed, and taking a deep breath dove in from the shore. Mid-air, my body tensed up in resistance to the anticipated shock of the icy snow-fed water. It seemed a natural thing to fear the loss of something we think we have. The flip side is discovering things we can't imagine having or experiencing. This was something I needed to work at – suppressing the fear of loss so that I might be open to the opportunity for something new and wonderful. As my fingers brushed the water's surface the tension in my body melted into surrender; to nature, uncertainty, and letting go of the control I'd claimed over my life.

Revolution and revelation; like the flooding rains settling into Kati Thanda, as I broke the surface the hollow void in my heart filled with the realisation that the existence of each truth, each family, didn't have to diminish the other. All those questions that swirled in my head – forces of nature and nurture, destiny and choice – didn't have to be framed as a zero-sum game pitting a truth against a lie. Released from the chains of this false dichotomy, I realised I didn't have to choose my 'real' father. Like G Cornucopia had explained in his history of Chaco Canyon, both stories are true.

I emerged from the freezing lake with my skin tinged with red blotches of stark invigoration and joined Gerry, who stood silhouetted against the fading sky, calmly drinking his cup of tea. A twilight beckoned of unnameable hue, with the blush of dusky sunset over mountain peaks reflected in the mirror-still water as twin images. As evening deepened and sunset slowly burnt the sky to darkness the far shore stayed visible as a thin silver line, vast and spacious, like sky and water merging. Such mystery awaited beyond horizon's view.

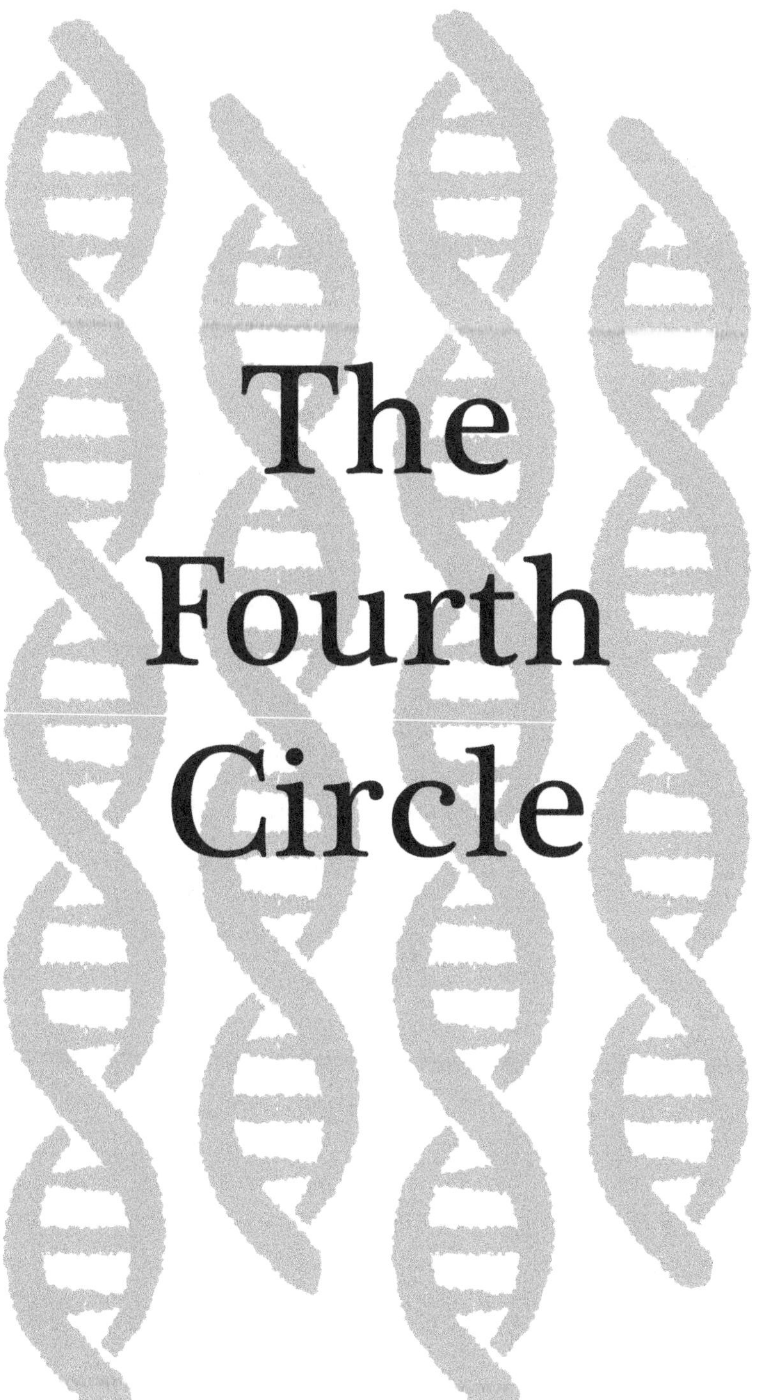

The Fourth Circle

Fifteen

Five years after first meeting Ben in Cape Paterson, Gerry and I drove towards another beach. It was two days after Christmas and our destination this time was Wapengo on the South Coast of New South Wales.

Gerry steered the car off the spotted-gum-lined road onto a dirt track at the top of a tidal inlet punctuated by small white posts marking oyster beds. The track meandered along beside the mangrove-fringed water on one side, rolling green hills on the other, until it reached a gate hung with a simple wooden sign that spelt out *Ness* in painted letters. The Old Norse *Nes* means a headland or promontory. As the sun descended behind dark clouds heavy with summer rain I got out to open the gate. We were almost at the end of a long eight-hour drive from Melbourne.

The dirt road snaked past a few gum trees and bushy banksias then forked in two. The left branch led to a public campground in the adjacent Mimosa Rocks National Park and the right fork was blocked by another gate that read, *No Entry, Private Property*. As

I undid this chain I felt a tiny bit nervous, like I was trespassing. I had made arrangements with Ben's brother Rowland, who lived nearby, to let him know we were coming, and Rowland had given me the phone number of Mick, the resident caretaker, to let him know our plans. I'd tried calling Mick a few times but hadn't managed to get through.

Beyond the second gate the road reached a reed-lined soak and stables made from wooden palings and corrugated iron. A chestnut horse with a white blaze on its forehead stood sanguinely behind the fence. A little further back a cottage sat nestled at the bottom of a hillside that sloped up to the bush. Scattered between the stables and cottage was a small herd of self-shearing sheep in various stages of shedding. Heads down, their furry white ears moving, they munched on the grass nourished by recent rain. A couple of black-and-white willie wagtails hopped between the sheep, waggling their tails as they hunted grubs.

'Maybe we should stop in to let Mick know we're here,' suggested Gerry.

I looked up at the cloud-filled sky. 'Let's get the tent up first before it starts raining. We can come back after.'

A little further along we pulled off the road at an embankment that led to a serene grassy camp site overlooking the inlet. On the far bank the coastal forest stretched from the beach to the foothills of Mumbulla Mountain. A white-bellied sea eagle stared at us from a nearby dead tree as I ferried armfuls of camping gear from the car to the camp site. I heard the sound of an engine above the chiming of the bellbirds and a tiny ute appeared over the rise. A man dressed in a flannel shirt, old trousers and a wide-brimmed hat hopped out of the cab and ran towards us, shouting and waving his arms.

'Who are you?! You can't camp here. This is private property.'

I froze. He was right; I wasn't supposed to be here. This had all been a terrible mistake. As he got nearer he regarded me closely and stopped waving his arms.

'Well, you're obviously a Clark,' he said.

I flushed, partly thrilled and partly uncomfortable to be so unfamiliarly recognised. If only he knew what heresy was embedded in his words. I wasn't sure what to say.

'I'm Lauren. And this is Gerry,' I ventured as introduction, praying he wouldn't follow up with a question about exactly what sort of Clark I was. I didn't have the words to answer awkward questions. 'I spoke to Rowland about camping, and tried to call you, but couldn't get through.'

His whole demeanour changed. 'G'day, I'm Mick. Rowland mentioned you'd be coming. The bloody phone's been on the blink. I've had the technician from Telstra out here three times already. I didn't mean to startle you. I have to keep an eye on things because we get campers sneaking in through the gate.'

'No worries,' I said, relieved. 'I understand.'

After Mick left we pitched our tiny hikers' tent amid the coastal forest of spotted gums, stringybarks and bangalays. After making up our bed we drove the last kilometre of the sandy track to a modest wooden house enclosed on three sides by a verandah. The building stood low on the point of land between the inlet and the ocean, almost hidden behind the banksias. Gerry parked our white station wagon beside a blue station wagon of the same vintage.

From speaking to Rowland I knew that this week between Christmas and New Year's was a busy time. Ben's three surviving brothers and only sister, Bas, Andrew, Rowland and Katerina, and a selection of their children and grandchildren were all staying on the property. I was about to meet the real-life people behind the potted family tree I had received in my first letter from Ben. That first contact was five years earlier, but I still felt the familiar nervous butterflies in my stomach.

'How am I going to introduce myself?' I whispered to Gerry as the icy hands of illegitimacy crept up my body. Who was I? An obscure bygone. An artificial bastard intruding on this family.

'You'll manage,' he whispered back encouragingly.

I made Gerry go first, using him like a shield as we walked in the back door. The room was warm and thrumming with the noise of a dozen strangers I had never met but shared genes with. My mind fogged with sensory overload as the kettle whistled, adults chatted and a man changed a baby's nappy on the floor near a large brick fireplace. Nearby more children played and drew pictures beside a red chaise longue. A broad-shouldered man with brown-grey hair looked over at me. His kind, blue eyes caught mine and instinctively I walked towards him.

'Hi, I'm Lauren. This is Gerry.'

'Welcome, you two. I'm Rowland. It's so fantastic to meet you both.'

A man walked over with similar features to Rowland, but slightly narrower eyes, bushier eyebrows and a familiar nose. Rowland introduced him as Andrew.

I shook his hand. 'Lovely to meet you. You're a journalist right?'

'Yes, I do the occasional scribble.'

As I was telling Andrew that I had thought about becoming a journalist when I was leaving school we were joined by their eldest brother, Bas, who lived in Melbourne, and their sister, Katerina, who'd travelled from her home in Connecticut. A pattering sound on the roof added to the orchestra of voices as the long-threatened rain began to fall.

'Would you like a wine?' offered Rowland.

I accepted gratefully.

'It's from my winery near Canberra,' he said, pouring Gerry and me each a generous glass.

I picked up the bottle of cabernet sauvignon to take a closer look. The label was inset with a black-and-silver photograph of two figures standing back to back, fishing from a jagged rock as a wave crashed into white foam. I recognised the figure on the left from the silhouette of his bush hat as Manning Clark. I wasn't sure about the other, although their fishing stance had a certain similarity.

As if reading my mind, a woman's voice said, 'That's my dad and Manning fishing from the rocks just off the point here.' I turned and unexpectedly found myself staring into my own blue eyes. Surreally, I watched my lips form the upturned welcoming smile of introduction. But this wasn't a mirror, or an out-of-body experience. It was Anna Clark. Ben had told me I reminded him of his niece when we first met all those years ago. In Germany they might have referred to us as *Doppelgängers.*

Kurt Gödel's ideas about the elusive truths contained within self-referencing loops influenced the Dutch graphic artist MC Escher, who created prints with ambiguous boundaries between different levels of reality. *Self-Portrait in Spherical Mirror* depicts a hand holding a mirrored sphere whose reflection reveals the hand belongs to Escher. I am you and what you see is me.

'Hi,' was all I could manage in bemusement as we shook hands. She was dressed in an old T-shirt and shorts and had a tall, athletic frame. Anna introduced me to her partner, Gab, who had finished changing the baby on the floor, and we started chatting about sports. She told me about playing Aussie Rules Football up to the age of fourteen, the only girl on the team. Gab chimed in that she had won the best and fairest award.

Like me, Anna had a PhD, although hers was in history. I wasn't a historian but I understood the compulsion to delve back into the past. Like Manning, Anna explored beyond the official versions of Australian history. Her work focused on who was deemed entitled to hold the pen, examining which sources were considered credible and authoritative, and which were absent from our history. Maybe it was okay to be interested in the blank spaces. Anna's scholarship went beyond the official documents of colonial history, elevating the stories of ordinary people as well as oral histories from Indigenous peoples as important historical sources.

With this whirlwind of introductions my head was starting to spin, but my brain clicked into social mode. I chatted brightly and nonchalantly, as if this was the sort of thing I was used to doing every day.

After a few hours we said goodbye and retreated back to our camp site where I tried to debrief my cluttered thoughts with Gerry.

'Isn't it amazing how many people in the Clark family have PhDs? Katerina and Axel, and Anna and her brother Tom,' I said, counting them off on my fingers. 'And Dymphna was studying for one. Before coming here I'd hardly met anyone with a PhD. Here it feels totally normal.'

Worn out from the long drive and the emotional energy of meeting so many new people, I fell asleep to the soothing rhythm of breaking waves. I woke during the night to find the clouds had cleared, revealing a clarity of stars. In the direction of the ocean, distant bolts of blue lightning flashed, without the sound of thunder.

The next day was a relaxed affair of book-reading punctuated by cooling swims. At one point I glanced up as a solitary black-and-white pelican with mohawked head and enormous fleshy bill flew over the water, thrust out its feet and made a splashy landing. It was low tide, and I admired the sandbars sculpted by forces of current, wind and storm that gave rise to a miraculous palette of colours somewhere between green and blue. Unveiled in all their glory by the sun, I tried to name the myriad hues with words like turquoise, cerulean and cobalt, but they were slippery, like the definition of where I fit into the Clark family.

We'd been invited to join the others for dinner at the house, where I felt history seeping out through the timber walls and blue-checked curtains. One of Manning's bush hats hung from a peg next to the kitchen. On the opposite wall a sepia portrait of a man and a woman in formal attire stared out at me from the past.

As we sat around a dark oval table in front of the brick fireplace, I heard the story from Bas, Rowland, Katerina and Andrew of how their mother, Dymphna, bought the property in the late 1960s with money from her inheritance. It was a failed dairy farm owned by two brothers whose wives didn't get along. The farmers had cleared the land around the inlet and caused an erosion problem. Dymphna, a very practical environmentalist, collected seeds from the native trees on the property to cultivate seedlings, which she planted all around the inlet. As the coastal forest took root, it stopped the soil eroding into the water. The animals, birds and fish returned.

After dinner Katerina asked me if I would like to go for a walk. Not far from the house we stopped to sit on a bench overlooking a rocky point at the mouth of the inlet. As the cloudy, humid sky diffused gold and pink sunset rays, a solitary black swan flew up the inlet, displaying white underwings. Katerina pointed out the gold plaque on the bench engraved with her brother Axel's name and years of his birth and death.

'Axel was an English lit academic. He'd written a book on the Australian poet Christopher Brennan and was giving a talk to the Brennan society when he suddenly collapsed. Some people thought he'd had too much to drink. The doctors found a tumour at the base of his brain in a very sensitive region that controlled breathing and blood pressure. He was in his late thirties.'

'Oh no.'

'They couldn't remove it completely, so he had to have radiotherapy. The tumour was slow growing, but over the years he had to have several more surgeries. Unfortunately, each time he lost more function. Eventually the cancer affected his short-term memory and he couldn't teach anymore.

'We scattered his ashes from the fishing rock,' explained Katerina, pointing out to the rocky outcrop. 'That's where Anna learnt to fish.'

Anna, with whom I shared an eerie resemblance. *I am you and what you see is me*. She had lost her father, Axel, when she was in her early twenties. And I … I wasn't sure how to describe what had happened to me at a similar age. On one level our experiences had been completely different. Yet somehow they felt connected by a thread of grief over something lost. But my experience didn't have a name and wasn't accompanied by rituals or social supports. There was nothing to commemorate it except for the plaque on St Kilda Road stamped with the Australian coat of arms and the impersonal logo of a property developer.

'Andrew also suffered the same type of brain cancer as Axel,' continued Katerina. 'He was staying here and went on a trail ride led by Mick. He lost his balance while the horse was walking on flat ground, fell, and broke his collarbone. Mick drove him to hospital in Sydney. The doctor investigated and discovered the brain tumour – it's called an ependymoma. Since the surgery Andrew has had problems with loss of balance – difficulty walking up stairs, that type of thing.'

Katerina and I walked down a steep staircase to the point. Carefully, we made our way around sharp-canted fins of rock to arrive at the sandy swimming beach.

'It was a really difficult time for the family,' Katerina continued. 'Mum had died the previous year, after being diagnosed with cancer. She decided not to have treatment. Instead she came here and swam every day. She really loved swimming across the inlet. We used to spend Christmas here every year, but after Mum's funeral, we didn't get together for quite a while.'

Later that night, lying in the tent, I thought about the cluster of brain tumours in Axel and Andrew, and wondered if I should call them my uncles. It was tricky. The words felt borrowed, like an ill-fitting suit. I recalled how unknown medical history wasn't very important to Rel before she was diagnosed with terminal bowel cancer. Should I be worried?

Sixteen

The holiday at Wapengo rolled on, with a cricket match and a relaxed bonfire party for New Year's Eve. On New Year's morning I pulled on some clothes and stumbled out of the tent in the pre-dawn. Grey light filtered down in gauzy rays through groves of casuarinas, spotted gums and spiky burrawangs as I walked the track to the house alone. The fresh morning air felt infused with a strong feminine energy. Today the coastal forest Dymphna had cultivated was home to countless living beings. Kangaroos and wallabies dashed, startled, into the undergrowth. Ancient, gnarled goannas loped past, using their sharp claws to climb trees.

At the clifftop above the beach east of the house I sat on a rickety plank balanced on two logs, listening to the silver trill of wrens and the rattle of wattlebirds. High above the water a pair of white-bellied sea eagles circled. I stared out at the ever-changing moods of the ocean. The tide was out, exposing the narrow channel between the rocks. The eastern sky was aglow above the dark water and three shafts of light slanted upwards from the unseen sun. As I walked down the steep track to the beach it appeared above the horizon, spreading a golden light that pierced the clouds. I undressed to the rhythmic roar of the ocean. Leaving my clothes in a neat pile on the sand I immersed myself in the cold, clear water. My skin awoke with a thousand sharp points that cleared away hangover and fatigue. The incoming swell formed enormous peaks that hung like skyscrapers and crashed fiercely onto jagged fins of rock in a maelstrom of white foam. But the narrow channel was surrounded by this protective ring of rocky reef. Feeling sheltered and safe from the breaking surf I dove under and propelled myself forward with dolphin kicks, my fingertips just brushing the edges of the channel. Overhead the sea eagles soared effortlessly on the breeze.

I surfaced and with a boom an incoming wave flooded the channel, propelling me back in towards the rock pools. As the saltwater began to drain back out, the undertow built and the outgoing current sucked me through the narrow aperture in the weed-clad rocks. My body responded with a rush of adrenaline and I began to swim with all my strength towards the shore, desperately trying to get back into the safety of the channel. I realised my flailing arms and legs were helpless against the power of the sea, which effortlessly swept me out beyond the protective reef.

Time slowed as the light from the dawn sun reflected, blinding, off the quicksilver ocean. *All they'll find will be that small pile of clothes* was the thought that bubbled up through my mind as the shoreline receded. Fighting against fate, I again thrashed with all my strength. With a surge an incoming wave lifted me up and swept me back in through the channel. The next moment, like a piece of flotsam, I unexpectedly arrived back on the beach, naked and dripping wet, with the roar of crashing surf ringing in my ears.

The sudden brush with death blew life into my face, sharpening my senses. My emotions were a mixture of exhaustion, elation, fear and awe. I stared below the tide line. The monster wave that had returned me to shore had erased my footprints, leaving no trace.

The shock of the near drowning shook something loose; the realisation that just as Gödel warned, my story is flawed by incompleteness. It's unavoidable in any tale of donor conception. The perceptive reader may have already sensed a gap, a blank space hovering between the lines, or perhaps even between the very letters on the page. I've tried to be as accurate as possible, but everyone involved has their own point of view, and my perspective isn't the only truth.

I'll admit that when I really want or don't want to do something, I can be selfish and uncompromising. Thinly disguised stubbornness digs in until my preference wins the battle of attrition. As I've recounted, I felt compelled to seek the truth of my provenance, wherever that led me. Part of this process was going public and reclaiming my agency by smashing the secrecy and lies that characterise donor conception. I hoped that telling my story would humanise the issues faced by donor-conceived people and help educate the public about why many of us seek access to information about our genetic heritage. I reasoned a shift in public opinion would in turn generate political pressure and momentum towards changing the law. I was completely driven towards this objective and couldn't stop.

Eventually, everything I'd hoped for came to pass, but speaking out had myriad consequences, like ripples on a pond.

I pulled my clothes back on over goose-pimpled flesh and walked back up the short path through the forested embankment towards the house. Suddenly I froze. My path was blocked by a magnificent diamond python, over two metres long. Its dark green, almost black, skin was emblazoned with lemon-coloured diamonds of various cuts and facets. The intricate geometry diminished fractally into tiny yellow dots the size of a single scale, like an Escher print. I watched in fascination as the snake navigated the distance between me and the steps leading up to the verandah in serpentine perambulations. It stopped and raised its head about a foot off the grass to survey me as its tongue flicked, tasting the air. Those cool, hypnotic black eyes contained a shared understanding.

I felt a strange sensation, a sort of deep itchiness. As I scratched at my arms, chunks of skin began to fall away. Alarmed, I tried to hold things in place. Despite my best efforts my skin began to peel away in long strips. Fighting the terror of what might emerge from underneath, I began to tear away my flesh. It came away in flaky handfuls and I felt a separation – the cutting of sinews that bind skin to muscle, and an opening up of my joints. I wondered if sensation would alter from the contours of my outer body to the inner one being revealed, and old fears flared. What if something went wrong after my outer skin had already cleaved and I discovered the new skin had failed? Would there be a moment of disconnect, of non-existence, when I could feel neither the skin that had been shed or the new-grown skin? Or perhaps I would feel both skins simultaneously, a blurring of boundaries, shifting shapes and ambiguous identities?

The snake finished shedding its skin. After resting a moment it slithered away and vanished beneath the house. I stooped down to pick up the old skin – dry and delicate – bunched up like a crumpled sock. The scales were textured like a thin plastic membrane imprinted with the tiniest details of the snake, even its eyes.

On our last morning at Wapengo, after pulling out pegs and poles and folding up the tent, I stopped to examine the tree I had just spent a week sleeping under. It was a bangalay, sometimes known as a bastard mahogany. As I placed my hand on the red-tinged, vertically furrowed bark I was reminded how from little things, big things grow. Dymphna, the practical environmentalist, created a living example, cultivating thousands of seedlings from the native trees on the property to regenerate the coastal forest we had camped under.

The bangalay's story is one of resilience. It is adapted to not only survive a fire, but to thrive. Fire brings many changes, but among them can be a blossoming. A tree burnt to the ground by bushfire often recovers in mallee form with one scorched trunk re-sprouting as many, not unlike my own family tree. But to notice only what happens above ground is to miss half the story. I'd also just spent a week sleeping above the tree's roots. These living buds hidden beneath the ground are the secret to how the bangalay can recover so miraculously from bushfire. But the trees can't survive without their roots entangled in the greater forest, their family.

After finishing packing up our camp site Gerry and I made our rounds across the property to say goodbye to all the wonderful people we had met over the past week.

'It was lovely to have you both here, really fantastic,' said Rowland as I kissed him goodbye. 'You're always welcome to stay here at Ness.'

'Thanks. We'd love to come back sometime.'

'I only ask that during Christmas and school holidays, times when it gets a bit busy, only family can reserve a place here.'

'Oh.' I kept my face neutral but inside I felt like an idiot. An interloper. All the events of the past week – the dinner, cricket match and New Year's Eve party – they had just extended the invitations to be polite to a guest. I stared down at the ground.

'That includes you,' chimed in Bas, who was standing nearby.

'Obviously,' said Rowland, enthusiastically.

'Definitely,' echoed Bas.

'Obviously! You belong to this place too.'

I smiled. 'Thank you.' And my heart stirred.

Like everybody, I'm a tangle of genes, psychology and experience, but with an extra layer of complexity to my family story.

In meeting and getting to know all of Ben's surviving siblings – Bas, Katerina, Andrew and Rowland – and most of my cousins, I've discovered our lives echo recognisable rhythms. There was something intensely satisfying in finally being able to make sense of so many things by seeing my looks, personality and interests mirrored in multiple generations. Like many in this family I have a PhD, drive a sensible station wagon, love nature, drop crumbs down my shirt, excel at sports and enjoy being irreverent.

Many of my traits were also inherited or taught to me by the parents I grew up with. As noted by Professor de Kretser, he chose C11 as a match for my parents because they were both educated, and they duly passed on a love of learning to my curious mind. There was a serendipitous compatibility in other core values I was exposed to in my upbringing. My mother often took me camping, where I fell into my own world, wrapped up in the wonders of nature. Like many in the Clark family, Mum and her twin sister, Joan, owned and rode horses. She too was good at maths and science, but being a female and working class in the times she grew up in she was strongly encouraged to drop those subjects. My dad taught me self-discipline in his role as my athletics coach, helping me develop a strong body and mind through sports. His support turned my dream of flight into a reality. He cultivated a competitiveness and a desire to win that helped me overcome the many obstacles I faced during my search. I was also helped by my stubborn determination, characteristic of my mother.

To conclude that the spur that propelled my search that resulted in meeting the Clarks was a desire to displace my own childhood, memories and identity, or a betrayal of the parents who raised me, is to fundamentally miss the point. New relationships shouldn't have to come at the cost of the old. There is no crisis of conflict, because love is not a finite resource. The exploration of these new family connections opened into an amazing, expansive journey. I feel incredibly lucky and grateful that the large extended Clark family has been without exception warm and welcoming, and I can hardly comprehend that all these people might not be in my life had the governor denied my request.

Yet, even though I got the best result I could have hoped for from my search, a shadow lurks. A part of me feels cheated, swindled out of the opportunity to grow up already knowing all the facets I am gradually discovering about myself. After Mum revealed the truth about me being donor conceived, I assumed the hazy figure that haunted my peripheral vision was C11, my unknown biological father. Perhaps it was really my shadow self, the alternative person I might have become growing up as a tree rooted to this greater forest of kinship connections, stories and history.

Seventeen

'Do you want to know a secret?' I asked my best friend Laura one afternoon as we played after school on the paved patio of her back yard. We were both about six years old.

'Yes.'

I pointed up towards the blue sky, 'If we climb up really high, and jump, we'll be able to fly.'

Her eyes widened incredulously. 'Really?'

I nodded. This was something I knew from my dreams.

After scrambling up a retaining wall I stepped onto the top of their brick barbecue. Laura followed suit. We faced one another.

'Ready?'

She nodded.

'Three, two, one, go!'

I bent my chubby little knees and jumped as high as I could, flapping my arms furiously in imitation of the flocks of cockatoos I'd seen flying over the street each evening before sunset. Arcing upwards, I waited for a cushion of air to catch me and sweep me up into the sky, as regularly happened in my dreams. Instead, my arc of movement began to turn in a distinctively downward direction. My knees bent to absorb the shock as I landed hard on the concrete pavers. To my left I saw that Laura had fared no better.

'It didn't work,' Laura said indignantly.

'It didn't work this time,' I corrected her. 'Maybe we didn't flap hard enough. Or jump from high enough. We just need to keep trying.'

As the years passed the desire to fly like a bird never left my subconscious, manifesting as recurring dreams of taking flight. I felt a deep connection between flying and the highest level of being: freedom.

It was my dad who helped turn my dreams into reality. When I was fourteen he investigated flying schools and drove me out to Essendon airport for an introductory flight. My inner dreamscape was displaced by the pungent fumes of aviation gasoline and the noise and vibration of a piston engine hurtling down the runway at full power. After take-off the world seen from the bubble canopy was made miniature. Thrillingly for a teenager who had never driven a car before, the instructor handed over control and let me steer the tiny two-seater aircraft. We bumped along, hitting small pockets of turbulence, floating above the city.

I walked back into the office grinning as Dad paid for the flight. He was generally averse to spending a lot of money, but helping his child fulfil her dream brought out a more generous side to his nature. He also bought me a navy-blue hardcover book with gold lettering – my pilot's logbook – in which I proudly recorded the details of my first flight.

From then on, once a month Dad drove me out to Essendon airport for more flights, all dutifully recorded in my logbook.

One summer's afternoon, after thirteen hours of lessons, my instructor hopped out of the aircraft and left me alone in the cockpit. With butterflies in my stomach I pushed the lever to full throttle. Unlike the barbecue attempt, this time I really did take off, from the south-facing runway, aluminium wings the avatar to my flapping arms. I scanned the airspace for traffic and swung the control column left, simultaneously stepping on the left rudder pedal, and the aircraft made a loping 180-degree turn. On the downwind leg I kept straight and level and completed my pre-landing checks. Reducing the throttle, I began to descend, pulled the handbrake-style lever to deploy the flaps and made the radio call for the turn onto final approach. As the runway loomed I aimed for the centreline, cut the engine and pulled back on the control column to flare for landing. The wheels touched down smoothly. Breathing hard, I braked and taxied off the runway to my waiting instructor. It was my sixteenth birthday.

In the following year my logbook records several flights to the Point Cook training area, and longer sorties around Victoria, practising navigation skills. I passed the test for my private pilot's licence in my final year of high school when I was seventeen years old and still not legally allowed to drive a car by myself.

The last flight entered in my logbook records that I flew as pilot-in-command with Dad as my passenger. We flew together for 0.9 hours from Essendon to Point Cook and back. Dad was thrilled. At last we were able to share in my dream that he had helped make real; the freedom of the sky.

Mum gave me a different kind of freedom. She taught me how to read before I started school and supplied me with a steady stream of interesting books that I duly devoured. At night I took a torch to bed so I could continue to read long after lights out. In grade one I wrote in my school diary, *Mum took me to see the movie* My Left

Foot. *It was good, but not quite as good as the book.* My teacher was sceptical but it was true. During the school holidays I had been bored so I'd read a copy of Christy Brown's autobiography. Mum didn't place restrictions on what I was allowed to read and books shaped my ideas, opinions and actions.

Perhaps the one time she regretted not limiting my reading was when I was thirteen and my cousin Kathryn lent me a book by Peter Singer called *Animal Liberation*, which detailed factory farming practices. I became a vegetarian.

From Green River Lakes, Gerry and I hiked down to the main campground and managed to hitch a ride in the back of a pick-up truck over the long, bumpy exit road. After interminable kilometres of rutted corrugations we returned to our starting point and joyfully reunited with the ever-loyal Tan Can.

Back on the road we drove south from Wyoming to Colorado and crossed the Rocky Mountains to the east side of the Continental Divide, where raindrops drained into the Atlantic Ocean. It was September and the autumn colours were arriving. Hillsides sported groves of aspens with neon-yellow and red leaves shivering in the wind. Following the interstate for several days through Nebraska and Iowa to Illinois, I composed a haiku.

Cornfields cornfields corn
Fields cornfields cornfields cornfields
Cornfields cornfields corn

Beyond Chicago we journeyed through Pittsburgh, upstate New York, Vermont, New Hampshire and Massachusetts, then south to Connecticut. At the end of this long journey Gerry parked the Tan Can in Ben's sister Katerina's driveway. It was nearly three years since that first trip to Wapengo. The two-storey house's steep-pitched grey shingled roof was fringed by majestic maples and oaks, slowly shedding brown and gold leaves.

The wooden front door was opened by Katerina's youngest son, Bas, affectionately known as 'Little Bas' to distinguish him from his admittedly shorter uncle. He greeted us and showed us in. The first thing I noticed was the books – piled high on every horizontal surface.

Bas showed us through to the kitchen. The house felt relaxed and comfortable. A sliding glass door led into an adjoining greenhouse with a pitched roof. Parsley, thyme, tomatoes and strawberries grew in planter boxes and pink geraniums hung from trellised hanging pots. In the dining room a small laptop occupied an island of space on a table piled comically high with academic papers. More geraniums grew in the dining-room bay window.

Katerina arrived home on her bicycle from Yale University where she was tenured as a professor specialising in twentieth-century Russian history and culture. In her early twenties, she spent two years living in Russia and learnt to speak the language fluently. Now in her seventies, Katerina was incredibly vigorous and kept fit cycling to and from work, even during the freezing Connecticut winters. Her twin passions were her job – researching, writing and teaching – and her family, especially horsing around with her grandchildren.

After quickly changing from practical work attire into a comfortable jumper and tracksuit pants, Katerina served up a pasta dish she'd prepared earlier, which we ate in the kitchen. On the wall opposite to where I sat was a colourful poster advertising

Manning Clark's History of Australia: The musical, which played in Melbourne as part of the 1988 Australian bicentenary celebrations. The poster depicted a line of cartoon characters from Australia's history linking arms and dancing in a row. Manning, in his iconic bush hat, held his then five-volume *A History of Australia* under his right arm. His left arm was draped around the shoulders of Queen Elizabeth II, who wore a purple dress and tiara and thrust a sprig of wattle high into the air. To Manning's right was Ned Kelly, a smile drawn onto his iron head armour. Everybody was kicking their left leg out to the right, except for Manning, who kicked his right leg out to the left.

The next morning Katerina got up at five to sit in her armchair redrafting her latest manuscript. Several hours later the rest of us were up and we all sat at the kitchen table to eat breakfast together. As Bas made a French press coffee Katerina told me a funny story about my biological father, 'Neddy'.

'Many years ago Neddy met me in Italy after his travels across the United States and Canada. We spent a couple of weeks making our way to France. At the Atlantic coast he swam from the beach far out into the ocean, eventually out of sight. He was a bit naughty and attempted to swim across the border into Spain. He was picked up by the border guards.'

Later, I emailed Ben to ask if this story was true, and he replied, 'Everything Katerina says is true. If our dad wanted to know what was happening in Canberra he would call up Katerina in New Haven.' I put this fresh charge to Katerina who retorted that because she was the only girl in the family her dad falsely assumed she was the gossip.

Before she left for work the two of us went for a walk and bumped into a neighbour. 'This is my niece visiting from Australia,' said Katerina, introducing me. In the past such familial language had made me feel uncomfortable – at best the words felt borrowed; at worst, illicit and stolen. But in my constantly evolving internal narrative something had shifted, and it no longer felt strange to be described as Katerina's niece. I realised that rather than me being the thief, perhaps the language had been stolen from me.

Katerina cycled off to Yale to teach a class and Gerry, Bas and I spent some time examining the photos displayed in the dining room. We laughed at Bas and his brother Nick's long hair and Anna's high school formal photo from the 1990s. A white-edged sepia print showed Manning and Dymphna with their six children, their partners and assorted grandchildren at Wapengo, assembled on the swimming beach. The women sat on the sugary white sand with ruffled, salt-stiffened hair. The men formed the back row all sporting beards, except for Andrew, who was clean-shaven. Ben held Tuppence the black dog. Manning stood in his bush hat, unsmiling, posed with his raised left leg resting on Dymphna's left shoulder. Dymphna grasped his foot, relaxed and smiling. Manning the public 'annoyer of conservatives' and Dymphna the private architect of the picturesque family sanctuary.

They say the past is a foreign country. As I'd travelled across the vast United States my past had bubbled up, urging to be explored. Were there answers to be found here in Connecticut? Could I somehow locate a piece of myself?

The next morning Katerina and I sat drinking green tea at the kitchen table as Gerry and Bas attempted the Sisyphean task of raking up the autumn leaves scattered across her vast backyard. Despite living in the US for over fifty years Katerina still resided on a green card, intentionally maintaining her Australian citizenship as a core part of her identity. She told me the story of her marriage to her American ex-husband, Michael, who had passed away a few years earlier.

'My visa was running out, so we were supposed to be married by a lawyer friend at nine in the morning, but he was late for work. The receptionist searched the building and found someone else who could marry us. This guy showed up, hunted around and dusted off the pages of the official ceremony. He said the words and it was done. Then Michael had to leave to teach a class. It was very romantic! I was left with the celebrant who brazenly asked for twenty-five dollars. I had to pay for my own wedding.'

I laughed. 'At least it was cheap!'

Drinking my tea, I looked out into the glass conservatory adjoining the kitchen. 'I like your greenhouse.'

'Oh yes, I enjoy gardening. Mum was a great gardener.' Katerina looked outside. 'The snow is coming soon and the cold will kill those geraniums, but the ones in the dining room will last a bit longer.' She sipped her tea. 'Dad died in late autumn at home in Canberra. After he took his last breath Mum went out into the garden and picked a geranium and placed it gently in his hand. That's why I like to grow them.'

My gaze was drawn to the window box in the dining room, touched by how Katerina remembered her parents by surrounding herself with delicate pink blooms that grew in spring and died in the frosts of winter.

Unlike the five facts about C11 contained within the non-identifying paperwork, this story, revealed as we sat together over tea – not controlled by government, doctors or parents – communicated something deeper about the essence of Dymphna and Manning's relationship. Coming late to the party (so to speak) after both their deaths, it was comforting to discover this unexpected reservoir of collective memory. Each story shared was like a small, polished bead, all of them scattered across a vast plain. Slowly and patiently, over many years, I collected them up from various people and threaded them back together into the three-looped chain of my being. Memories regrafted, like roots on a tree.

Beginning with childish attempts to fly and, later, more serious efforts to attain my pilot's licence, all my life I had been exploring different manifestations of freedom. After learning I was donor conceived the journey turned inwards as I attempted to navigate the confused entanglement of memory and identity, past and present.

My outer journey of *Wanderlust*, ditching job and possessions for time to meander around the US, had made me realise that, just like the highways in the Southwest align with faults and breaks in the rock, the values that inform our thoughts and actions follow invisible cultural and historical signposts. I'd arrived at the fundamental question: who penned my history? Was it the state who issued my birth certificate and passed legislation that mandated irrebuttable paternity? (Donor-conceived people are the only cohort in Australia who cannot petition their birth certificates because by law they are irrebuttable.) Was it the clinic staff who deliberately destroyed or absentmindedly lost donor records? Was it my parents who didn't tell me the truth? Was it the online trolls and armchair experts who poured out their vitriol when I went public to call for a change in the law?

Who controls the past controls the future.

By strange loops of thought and action my inner and outer journeys had converged here in Katerina's kitchen where I found freedom in knowing I could one day grow geraniums in my own garden, imbued with a sense of meaning. A gift I would have been poorer never to have received.

That evening after dinner we retired to the living room. Katerina crouched in front of her stone fireplace on a deep burgundy Persian rug beneath a series of Indonesian shadow puppets pinned to the wall. Souvenirs from her own *Wanderlust*. Browsing the crowded bookshelves, I discovered they were filled with Clark literary endeavours. It wasn't just Manning's six-part opus, or Katerina's academic blockbusters, but the entire Clark family clogging the shelves: everything from poetry to biography to political analysis.

'She was very proud of it,' commented Katerina, as I flipped through the thick volume of Dymphna's greatest professional work, the translation from German to English of Baron Charles von Hügel's 1833–34 *New Holland Journal*. The diary chronicled the baron's travels across Australia, recording observations of flora and fauna, the British administration, Sydney society, missionaries, convicts, and Indigenous people he had met.

'Mum embarked on it after Dad died,' continued Katerina. 'Translating the book brought together her love of German, nature and Australia. She was very much in love with Dad, but her parents were crestfallen that she didn't continue with her PhD after she married him. Mum said she never wanted a career, but I wonder if she was a bit disingenuous.'

'She sounds like an amazing person. I would have liked to have had the chance to meet her.' A small silence hung in the air. 'I speak a bit of German too,' I continued. 'I've always felt drawn to the language. Not sure why.'

'Mum's father, Augustin, was from Belgium. His surname was Lodewyckx and he taught Germanic languages at the University of Melbourne. Mum's mother, Anna, had a Nordic background and taught Swedish there too. Her maiden name was Hansen.'

'When I travelled overseas people sometimes asked me if I was from Sweden,' I mused. 'When I found out that Dymphna had Scandinavian heritage it made a lot of sense.'

Gerry, Bas, Katerina and I passed the evening in comfortable silence around the fire, reading. Like the canoe that carried us down the Green River, the books on Katerina's shelves were another kind of time machine, transmitting ideas and memories across vast expanses of space and time. I pulled a blanket around my legs and opened up Dymphna's brother Axel Lodewyckx's book, *The Funding of Wisdom*. He described the twist of fate of how their family settled in Melbourne. En route from the Congo to Belgium, they were caught by the outbreak of the First World War in Australia. Stranded, their father Augustin accepted a post at the University of Melbourne and eventually decided to stay.

Katerina got up from her armchair and switched on the kettle. The water boiled and she poured it into a hot water bottle with a tartan cover, then popped her head into the living room to say goodnight. A while later I put the books back and stood up to go to bed. Turning back, I stared at the two white bookcases. When I finished high school I wasn't sure how to resolve my dual love of numbers and words. I received top marks in English, but didn't know anybody who was a journalist or a published author. I loved to fly, so chose the path of aeronautical engineering. That night in Katerina's living room I reflected on my choices in a different light, and dared ask myself a question: could I be creative?

Seeing the combined weight of the Clark family oeuvre on Katerina's bookshelves, I finally felt the confidence that writing was something I could do. Shortly afterwards, harnessing the scripturient desire that had awoken inside me on our travels, I picked up my pen and began the task of writing my own history.

Eighteen

After our nine-month *Wanderlust* around the United States, Gerry and I drove over the Golden Gate Bridge to sell our trusty steed to a woman from Santa Rosa who was planning a trip down the Baja peninsula. I cried as we said goodbye to the Tan Can, farewelling the end.

We returned to Australia for Christmas and Gerry resumed work in January. With no particular home to return to we housesat in various places around Melbourne for five months. In Seattle, I'd met the CEO of an early-stage start-up designing a hybrid-electric plane. We kept in touch and eventually he invited me to join the team, so I moved back to the US. As the start-up only had six months of funding it didn't seem sensible for Gerry to quit his job, so I moved alone. But the funding uncertainty dragged out for more than a year. Separated by the Pacific Ocean, Gerry and I made do with occasional visits and the time apart eventually put a strain on our relationship. Gerry told me he was sick of living in suspended animation and he was right. My existence had an uncertain, rootless quality: living on a short-term visa, working a fragile job, and calling Seattle my temporary home.

The start-up failed to secure more financing and fell apart in slow motion. After more than two years of untethered living, I was overdue to come home.

In the midst of packing up my life to prepare to return to Melbourne I opened an email from Ben. I stared at the computer screen in complete shock at what he had written.

I have some bad news – I have an ependymoma – the same very slow growing, very low malignancy, very awkwardly located brain tumour as Axel and Andrew.

I couldn't believe the cancer had struck for a third time. My thoughts flew to Rel.

Two weeks later I flew across the Pacific Ocean through the warp of space, time and seasons that is international travel and landed back in Melbourne to reunite with Gerry.

Shortly after getting back I met up with Ben's eldest brother, Bas, for coffee in North Melbourne. Afterwards he took me for a walk to the University of Melbourne. Bas pointed to a sun-drenched sandstone nook in the north-east corner of the Old Arts building, occupied by a large potted tree.

'This is the place where in 1934 a young woman used to enjoy sitting in the sunshine to read her books. A young bloke used to pass by and noticed her sitting there. It took him a few weeks before he worked up the courage to talk to her. They started chatting and realised they had something in common – both had found the Latin course covered what they'd already learnt at school, so they didn't attend the lectures.'

The beginning of Manning and Dymphna's relationship was

revealed after the ending. Together with Katerina's story of how they were parted through death, I had located the bookends on a marriage that lasted fifty-two years and produced six children, including my biological father. It should have been impossible for me to discover these stories. Yet somehow I had found them, or they had found me.

After saying goodbye to Bas, I walked the short distance to visit my old friend and comrade Pauline in Parkville. As we sat around the table that once served as TangledWebs's HQ, Pauline told me about the recent death of her dear friend Bernadette.

'I visited Bern a few weeks ago at her home in a residential unit in East Melbourne. She was unconscious and receiving palliative care. I said a last sad farewell and thanked her again for her role in helping Rel meet and know her father.'

'What do you mean?' I asked.

'Bern worked as an archivist at the Public Record Office for many years. It was her who came across the old Prince Henry's Hospital records stored there after the clinic relocated to Monash. She recognised their significance and alerted me to their existence. It was only through Bern's awareness that it was possible to locate the records relating to Rel's biological father, T5, and release them to the Attorney-General's Office.'

It flowed from what Pauline was saying that Bernadette's actions had also led to me connecting with Benedict, the gateway to a whole web of relationships such as this day spent with my uncle Bas. By recognising the worth of those fragile paper records Bernadette had achieved something extraordinary, but the deeds of women like her so often go unrecorded.

Ironically, Pauline explained, Bernadette had lost her own memory to dementia. It was a disease of slow violence, hollowing-out and eventual effacement. When you erase someone's memories, you erase their identity. 'Show me Eternity, and I will show you Memory,' as Emily Dickinson said.

Consciousness exists within the entanglement of our past and present. We are beings of time. But the string of remembered moments that constitute our 'I' don't just exist inside our own heads. Assuming the form of stories, they are woven into the lives of family, friends, and sometimes people we will never meet.

And so I understand the urgency that drove Manning to write his vision of Australia's history and why, weeks before his death, Axel launched the second volume of his biography of Henry Handel Richardson. There's a mortal compulsion to stow pieces of ourselves in places that will outlive our fragile bodies. Just like Rel lives on in the reverberating influence of the causes she campaigned for. A little of her essence remains within the safekeeping of the people whose lives she touched, including my own.

My discussion with Pauline about the Prince Henry's records stirred thoughts about my three donor-conceived half-siblings. All I know is there was a man born in December 1981, a woman born in August 1981 and a man born in July 1984, all to separate families. I can only wonder if I will ever know anything about them. Are they healthy and happy? A decade and a half since I first learnt of their existence, none has joined the Voluntary Register, or popped up on a DNA-testing database. At times I scan faces as I walk down the street, searching for them. Maybe they aren't even aware they are donor conceived. There are no accurate statistics, but it is estimated at least ninety per cent of donor-conceived people of my generation have not been told the truth of their origins. This doesn't mean they will never find out. It was impossible for the authorities and institutions to make a clean job of erasing the past. Something always remains.

To comprehend why so many parents continue to lie it's important to understand the first and greatest myth embedded within the very name 'assisted reproductive *treatment*'. The doctors who ran the donor programs never cured any man of his infertility, yet laws were amended to pretend they had. Donor conception is more accurately a system of assisted reproductive *substitution*. The real problem solved by artificial insemination by donor wasn't male infertility, but the social stigma of how a married woman could be impregnated with another man's sperm. At its heart it is a psychological treatment as much as a physical one. The technology required is minimal, such that it can successfully be done at home with kitchen utensils. The real innovation was embedding it within a clinical setting. Attending a hospital to be seen by a doctor in a white coat created enough psychological distance that it became if not palatable, then at least acceptable. This clinical coldness was required as an antidote to the intimacy of a sexual relationship. The unspoken theoretical basis of donor conception was if you could destroy all intimacy in the act of procreation, you could dissolve the parent connection. I can almost see those pioneering doctors who set up the donor programs rolling their eyes, wondering why us renegade miracle babies, now all grown up, still don't get it. Sex = parent. No sex = not parent. It's all so simple. For the offspring of genius medical students, we sure are a bit slow.

But despite the innovative medical framing, artificial insemination by donor was still a precarious 'treatment', particularly from a legal perspective. Rather than taking a path of honesty and seeking social licence for this means of family creation, the chosen approach was to embed the system in a bedrock of secrecy. Forced to mimic the narrow constraints of the socially acceptable nuclear family, clinicians gave donors codenames, and made attempts to match their physical characteristics to the infertile parent. Consent forms promising secrecy were signed. What little information they recorded was often later intentionally destroyed. Birth certificates still only allow two parties to be named, so the Family Law Act was amended to reflect intention and extinguish the relevance of genetic ties.

The architecture of donor conception was set down like one-way glass, so people like me would never be able to see through back to our conception story. But despite all these efforts, the secrets leached out anyway. Some donor-conceived people were told the truth by their parents or other family members, while others sensed their difference or discovered hidden documentation. Consumer-DNA testing and new laws that enable donors to seek contact with their donor-conceived children means the truth has multiple avenues to come out, independent of parental control. I've heard several stories from people who made the discovery they are donor conceived by logging into a DNA-testing website or reading a registered letter. By all accounts it is a shocking experience. For parents of donor-conceived people, the lie might be sweet in the beginning, but can taste bitter in the end.

Promising would-be parents a cure for their infertility is an extremely appealing way of framing the process, a powerful myth that invites them to exclude the relevance of the donor from their family unit. When artificial insemination by donor was only available to married heterosexual women, this frame was reinforced by various means. Standard practice was to select a donor whose physical characteristics matched the infertile man. Doctors often advised the couple to go home and immediately make love to introduce a psychological salve. Sometimes the same result was accomplished by mixing sperm from the infertile husband together with that of the donor before the insemination. No matter how it was done, the goal was to introduce an element of doubt that the donor was responsible for any subsequent pregnancy and therefore make it easier to believe the child was biologically the social father's. Many parents almost convinced themselves this was the case and to some degree buried the truth.

Reassured by the myth, and the existence of a real child, men could avoid difficulties such as dealing with the grief of their own infertility, potential shame from a belief that virility is intrinsically linked to masculinity, or jealousy stirred by their wife being impregnated with the sperm of another man. It was also convenient to recruit donors under the umbrella of the narrative that they were merely gift-givers and had no further role to play. Another advantage of this myth was it allowed the couple to hold on to the fantasy that the child was the same one they originally dreamt of creating, together. Almost forgetting about the existence of the donor, or being reassured they played a very minor role, helped justify the decision not to tell their child the truth.

At this point it was necessary to introduce an element of doublethink, as fear of the strength of the genetic connection was also a powerful motivator for secrecy. A common fear that prevents parents from being honest with their children is worrying that they might reject the non-biological parent. It was and still is commonly proclaimed that donor anonymity is a necessary condition to avoid disturbing the sanctity of the family unit. In reality, I have never heard of a donor-conceived person rejecting their social parent purely because they don't share genetics. For those parents with the courage to tackle late disclosure, such as my mother, the truth can be bitter in the beginning, but sweet in the end.

My observation is that the impact of disclosure on the relationships between family members is highly dependent on the level of shared or divergent beliefs in these narratives just discussed. It also gives some context as to why so many parents are at least initially uncertain or unsupportive of their child's decision to search for information about their donor. The intimately held wish or belief of the non-genetic parent that the child is really biologically theirs may become threatened when that child seeks information about or meets their biological donor parent. In some cases, for both parents acknowledging the donor's existence is akin to ripping off a scab to uncover a painful wound beneath. Some wholeheartedly resist facing this pain by using threats and emotional manipulation to try to retain control, which of course only adds to the burden on the donor-conceived person trying to navigate their situation. In my own case my connection with the Clarks has on occasion sparked my mother's jealousy. She's told me that sometimes she wishes she did not have to 'share me' quite so much with them.

As well as impacting on the relationship between donor-conceived people and their parents, shared or divergent world views concerning frames and narratives of family are also hugely impactful on the connection between siblings. Some donor-conceived people attach a significance to people they share genes with but didn't grow up with. I felt compelled to seek answers to my many questions. For others, the lack of social bonds in the context of donor conception does not come even remotely close to crossing the threshold called family.

To add extra complication, these responses are not clear-cut and static, but nuanced and often change over time. Some people start in one camp and slowly cross over to the other, or are simply lost in a fog of confusion, unsure of what they think. For donor-conceived people who view the family they grew up with as complete and whole, they may see their sibling who searches and reaches out to the donor family as an interloper who has selfishly created a disruption causing them and their parents unnecessary angst. Two different world views on the definition of family, held clearly and distinctly by siblings, can become irreconcilably separate. It might well be the case that each desperately wants the other sibling to join them in their world. But their brother or sister can't do this without violating their own beliefs – deeply grooved, like the highways in the Southwest – and so they can only watch one another from afar, separated by an uncrossable gulf. Over time, there can be a further divergence as the branches of each sibling's family tree regrow into different shapes.

Often, the only solutions that enable each sibling to live in accordance with their own world view are to agree not to speak about the subject, or to break off the relationship in a secondary fragmentation. Very sadly, I know donor-conceived twins who don't speak anymore, and many other cases of siblings whose relationships were damaged or broke down such that they have strained or no contact.

It seems cruel to have to face the choice of damaging something precious in order to begin new relationships – a strange and painful loss that can form the private backdrop to all the new connections gained. This is but a snapshot of the complexities a donor-conceived person might deal with as they attempt to navigate new and old relationships within their personal definitions of family, particularly when they begin from a position of secrecy and anonymity. Even where the outcome of a journey of search and outreach is generally positive it is likely to flare up accusations of divided loyalties from the family they grew up with. Managing the expectations of others can make a donor-conceived person feel like they are walking a tightrope in heavy winds. Keeping everybody happy is often incompatible with integrating their own personal definitions of family and identity, meaning a choice must be made about whether they meet the needs of themselves or loved ones. This decision is always fraught.

The dominant story about assisted reproductive treatment has always focused on the journey to parenthood, with the birth of the child presented as the happy ending. Thus, the person created is only seen in relation to others' perspectives. The parent or parents see a longed-for 'miracle baby' that makes their life complete. The doctor sees overjoyed parents and a triumph of scientific research. These medical high priests still can't or won't admit the problems they caused, as documented by the Victorian parliamentary inquiry, in the way they wielded God-like powers to create life.

The donor is the most mysterious party. Perhaps the sperm donor sees his altruistic hand gesture as just a gift, no different from donating blood? Amid this troika of perspectives society rarely stops to ask: how might the miracle baby see themselves? One legacy of being a miracle baby is even as an adult I'm still introduced as a 'child' conceived through assisted reproductive treatment – as if my adult life is a mere postscript to my true purpose. Perennially infantilised, we are often marginalised from the policy decisions that underpin our lives.

Ultimately the system of assisted reproductive treatment is there to produce a baby. The combination of people blinded by baby blinkers – the powerful emotional desire for a child at any cost –

coupled with the power of fast-evolving technologies makes for profit-driven big business. Australia has effectively banned anonymous donors as detrimental to the wellbeing of donor-conceived people and outlawed commercial trading in eggs and sperm to prevent exploitation of people's reproductive capabilities. However, this hard-won progress, opposed by vested interests, is under constant threat. In many other countries, including the United States, most of Europe and Asia, anonymous and commercial donor conception continues to be the industry norm. The very word *donor* is itself a bit of a misnomer because most people who supply their gametes are paid, often relatively large sums of money. Even in Australia the industry walks a fine ethical line between reasonable reimbursements and baby trading.

My understanding of these matters has been a long and ongoing journey. Over many years, I met and conversed with other donor-conceived and adopted people like Rel, Myf, Damian, Kim and Pauline and slowly climbed, like Alice, through the one-way looking glass constructed by the assisted reproductive treatment industry into the world that lay beyond. I found a stable definition of parenthood no longer exists, as all elements of conception and birth have been made slippery so they can be conveniently reversed, depending on intent. For example, if a woman needs to use donated eggs to conceive, then of course society and the law see her as the true mother because she has carried, nurtured and given birth to the child. And yet if a woman needs to use a surrogate mother, then of course society and the law says that the woman who contributed the DNA that created the child is the true mother, because the other woman was merely a 'gestational carrier'.

The laws governing assisted reproductive treatment are moving society towards a norm that intention is a prerequisite for parenthood.

This would mean only those who intend to become parents are legally recognised through parental rights and responsibilities. But outside the clinical assisted reproductive treatment system, there's a burgeoning number of women seeking sperm donors informally via the internet. In these forums sometimes there is the suggestion of, or agreement to, 'natural insemination', i.e., sex. Why should a man who participates in a sexual encounter that is expressly for the purpose of conception be deemed a donor and not a parent? If the means of insemination are changed from natural to alternative, does this make a difference? Could a man who has a one-night stand that accidentally leads to a pregnancy, who had no intention of conceiving, also argue against being deemed a parent? Is this fair to the child created?

During my three years as a board member for the Victorian Assisted Reproductive Treatment Authority (VARTA), I saw some tortuous logic in regard to commercial trading. For example, it is illegal in Australia for intending parents or clinics to offer or give 'valuable consideration' (payment) to donors in exchange for the 'goods' of their eggs or sperm. Yet it is perfectly legal for intending parents to give payment to a broker for 'third-party services' to procure the same eggs and sperm. Often these brokers sign up vulnerable donors in poor countries by offering exploitative payments beyond the reach of Australian law.

One of the most exhausting and disappointing aspects of my advocacy work has been the constant need to defend our altruistic system from these ever more creative attempts at commercialising the industry, and the resulting pressure on governments to shift to free-market self-regulation. When I was conceived, my mother's treatment was fully subsidised, but these days assisted reproductive treatment is big business. Clinics are furiously lobbying for structural changes pioneered by manufacturing in the 1980s; namely, permission to slash costs by leveraging 'global supply chains'. Parents want the best for their children, but decisions made now to source gametes from overseas for reasons of cost or expediency can terribly undermine their future child's long-term best interests and inadvertently fuel exploitation and human trafficking. A donor-conceived man I know was so psychologically impacted by this feeling of being a 'commodity' or product that he got a barcode tattooed on the side of his neck.

In response to this industry push the Victorian government released the Gorton report, which recommended that eggs and sperm originating from overseas countries such as Ukraine, South Africa and the US be exempted from independent scrutiny and important regulations that apply domestically, with the stated goal being to 'make access to treatment cheaper and faster'. If implemented, this will mean another disenfranchised generation of donor-conceived people. For them, facing massive geographic, cultural and language barriers, knowledge of their donor beyond the most rudimentary details will be all but impossible. Local and known donors offer more realistic prospects of a meaningful relationship.

Despite our problems, Australia is far in advance of the United States. Florida's legislature considered a fertility fraud bill that would make it illegal, among other things, for doctors to inseminate their patients with the doctor's own sperm (currently not a crime there). The bill also included provisions requiring fertility clinics to develop sperm storage best practices and submit to annual health inspections. The American Society for Reproductive Medicine and the Society for Assisted Reproductive Technology co-authored a private letter to state representatives that read, 'The requirements of the bill will only add costs to the provision of health care involving assisted reproduction,' and, 'Should the language remain intact as it is, we will have no choice but to publicly oppose SB 698'. Those clauses designed to protect the health and welfare of donor-conceived people were ultimately stripped from the bill.

All this points to a larger problem. When I started to learn German it shone a light on the power of language to direct ideas and concepts. Year on year, the language of market thinking has crept into every facet of human existence, powering the global trend towards industries influencing governments to regulate for their own profit. But a regulatory paradigm distilled through this prism is not appropriate for the assisted reproductive treatment industry because the creation of human life is not a consumer product or a commodity. It's essential that the conversation around policies and regulation abandons the language of the market to allow us, the people conceived, to reclaim our humanity.

Nineteen

Almost fifteen years after my mother's shocking revelation, I drove a now familiar route two hours south-east of Melbourne. As the highway crested the hill above Kilcunda and the spacious vista expanded over the Bunurong coastline, I felt the same thrill of reaching escape velocity. Unlike the first nerve-wracking visit to meet Ben in Cape Paterson all those years ago, this time I felt comfortable to drive myself. From Wonthaggi, I zigzagged to the heathlands and parked at the end of a gravel track under a gum tree. Ben was following just behind and parked his white ute nearby.

'Good to see you,' I said as we hugged in reunion. I'd been away in the US for over two years.

'Yes, you too.'

'I'm impressed you left the house for a bushwalk without wearing shoes,' I said, pointing to his naked feet.

'I've only stood on a snake once,' quipped Ben. 'I felt it wrap around my bare foot. It sounds strange but it actually felt quite nice. Soft and warm. I kicked and it went flying into the bush.'

I laughed.

We set out in the sunshine on a walking track that wound through the dense stands of tea-tree, banksia, casuarina and manna gums that sprouted from the ancient sand dunes. It was early spring and the wattle was in full bloom, covered in sprays of cheerful yellow puffs. As we walked, I realised that all the years of visits to the region had manifested as more than a deepening relationship with Ben and my half-siblings. In the clarity of my long absence overseas, I felt a sense of affinity with this landscape.

'How was America?' Ben asked.

I gave him a brief rundown of the trials and tribulations of the start-up I'd worked for in Seattle.

'I was never quite sure what happened; if there was sabotage, negligence or just bad luck.'

'The real answer is some questions have no answer,' commented Ben, dryly.

We avoided talking about his illness. Instead, I picked a sprig of brilliant yellow wattle and placed it in his shirt pocket.

'How's your mum?' Ben asked.

'She's good. I think she's happy to see me back in Australia.'

'You reckon? Or at least she's putting up a good front.'

I laughed. 'I think she loves Gerry more now than she loves me. I've been replaced.'

'Rightly so.'

As Ben bent down to adjust his cuff the sprig of wattle fell out of his pocket and tumbled to the ground. Before he straightened back up, he picked it up and returned it to his pocket. I felt strangely pleased.

Ben seemed so normal, even healthy. It reminded me of when Rel first got sick. Then, as now, it was hard to comprehend the reality. As we walked side by side down the bush track past a grove of manna gums we didn't have to meet each other's eyes. I decided to broach what had remained unspoken.

'So, you've been having some … issues with your health?'

'Yes. I haven't been feeling too well. It's hard to describe. A bit wonky and off-balance. I got a scan. The next day they called and said I had to come in to discuss the results. I thought – this doesn't sound good.'

'Yeah.'

'I went in and was told it's an ependymoma. Same as Axel and Andrew.'

'Epen-dy-moma,' I repeated slowly. 'It seems extraordinary that three brothers all had the same type of rare brain tumour. Could it be a coincidence, or is there a genetic link?' I asked casually, feeling slightly awkward.

'A few papers in the literature observe family clusters, which means there could be something, or maybe in the environment. Again, the real answer is some questions have no answer.'

I was already familiar with this realm. Questions without answers. Truths unprovable.

'The surgeon assessed me as Cat 1 for immediate surgery. It's this Friday. I should be in hospital for about a week.' Clouds had gathered to obscure the sun. 'The surgery has a one to two per cent chance of death. And a higher chance of serious side effects, such as permanent disability.' Ben paused. 'I can talk openly about all this because it feels like it's happening to someone else. I feel like I'm talking about someone else.'

I recognised that disembodied feeling. Shock.

The conversation drifted to other topics and I told him about my first experience of cross-country skiing, while living in Seattle.

'I'd like to try it again,' I said. 'Maybe an overnight snow camp next winter with Gerry. You should come with us.'

A slight shadow passed over Ben's face.

'How about this: I'll come if I'm able to, after the operation.'

I smiled. 'That sounds fair.'

The track opened up to the beach, revealing an expanse of sky, water and sand. I breathed in the salt tang. The sea was glassy but to the south dark water reflected storm clouds. Further out to sea the sun pierced through a small gap and shone down an arrow of silver light so brilliant I couldn't look directly at it.

On the beach I took off my shoes and socks and threw them aside to join Ben's barefoot party. I waded in to feel the temperature of the water and grimaced as the incoming wave immersed my bare feet.

'Still cold.'

I scrunched sand between my toes and showed Ben the tan lines on my brown feet from my recent northern hemisphere summer.

'My feet are getting a few wrinkles,' said Ben, pointing down. We both had solid big toes with the same ratio to the length of our second toes.

'Maybe you should get Botox?' I joked.

'Yeah, I don't want to be embarrassed about my bare feet as they wheel me into theatre.'

'I think you need to examine your medical priorities. Brain surgery can wait!'

Humour was the best deflector.

Walking west up the beach, the kelp swirled across a rocky reef exposed by the low tide. I detected a subtle drop in temperature and pressure as the storm front moved in. Dramatic clouds formed a dark purple montage punctuated by textured curtains of distant rain. Closer to shore, a concentrated golden sunbeam threaded through the moody grey sky directly ahead.

We stopped and stared out to sea, mesmerised by the speed of the rushing clouds. I tried to predict the path of the approaching storm. Were we going to get hit? The mood heightened as a strong wind blew in from the south-west and the sea surged up the beach. The glassy water began to crash with rhythmic waves and there was a sudden flash over Phillip Island.

'Did you see that?' I asked, pointing towards the afterglow.

Ben nodded. 'I think it's time to head back.'

We retraced our footprints along the beach. I picked up my shoes and socks but didn't put them on, testing if my soles were tough enough to walk the coastal scrub track barefoot. As we crossed the dunes, I felt the splash of a raindrop on my hand. The tea-tree lining the track formed a partial cave, like a bowerbird's nest, but it didn't protect us from the cold rain that was getting heavier, soaking my long grey tunic and black leggings.

'Think I'll run a bath tonight and get all cosy,' I said lightly, belying no concern, but I started to walk faster, worried that Ben might pick up a cold before his surgery. Perhaps we shouldn't have ventured out. The path got rockier and I stepped onto the grass edging. My feet were so cold I could barely feel the sharp rocks anyway. With relief I saw the metallic flash of cars. We were almost back. Over the last hundred metres of the track I thought about what I wanted to say, and even practised it in my head. Just as we crossed the threshold of the gate back into the car park the rain stopped.

I turned to face Ben. 'I know it's going to be a tough few days for you. I hope it goes really well – and it's not too stressful, even though I know it will be.' Well, that was garbled. 'Will you still be under anaesthetic on Friday?'

'Yes, I'll still be out of it. Probably for the next few days. Why don't you come visit me in the hospital on Monday?'

'Yes, I'll do that.'

'That'd be great.' He paused. 'I just hope I don't wake up a Collingwood supporter.'

I laughed. Ben was an ardent Carlton fan, their fiercest rival. 'Don't worry, if that happens, I'll pull the plug for mercy.'

There was another fleeting pause.

'Well, I won't let you stand around in the cold too much longer.'

We hugged.

'It was really good to see you,' said Ben.

'Yes. Let's do more of it. Should be easier now we're both in the same country.'

So much hung above the conversation, left unsaid. To add to the poignancy neither of us had acknowledged that today was Father's Day.

'I'm really glad we caught up.'

Ben's expression and tone of voice conveyed more than his words. I read the message in his eyes and felt happy.

'Me too. See ya.'

There isn't a dictionary in the world that contains a word to describe our connection to one another. Even German doesn't have a word for this relationship.

I woke up early on the morning of Ben's surgery and lay in bed listening to magpies carolling and the rain drumming on my mother's tin roof. Ben was first on the surgical list and had probably already reported to the hospital. I wondered how he felt – the doctor-turned-patient waiting for the orderly to wheel him into theatre and the medical team to spring into action.

At odd times during the day I remembered that Ben was lying under anaesthetic somewhere in the Royal Melbourne Hospital with people rummaging around inside his head. It felt abstract and unreal. I'd asked Charlotte to let me know when there was news so there was nothing further I could do except inhabit the uncertainty. For me the day went on and on, but for Ben it would be a timeless and dreamless sleep.

By four o'clock I hadn't heard anything so I texted Charlotte. She said the surgery was still going, she hoped good things were happening and she would update me. I sat staring out the window, thinking about the pressure on the surgeon to perform. The tiniest slip could cause severe disability or death. At 4.22 pm the rain suddenly stopped and the sun came out. At five there was a fierce hailstorm. Then at six the sky brightened into a golden sunset.

Still no news. It was nine o'clock. Surely the surgery must have finished by now. I checked my phone. No messages. I went to bed early and after some hesitation, turned off my phone. I knew that if I left it on each email alert would wake me. There was nothing I could do. I woke up at 4.30 am and switched my phone back on. Nothing.

Around 7.30 am I received a message from Charlotte that the surgery had gone well, but it was an incredible ordeal and his recovery was likely to take longer than expected. A wave of relief washed over me, together with admiration for the extraordinary surgeon. She had operated for ten intensely focused hours.

Poor Charlotte must have had a terribly stressful time. She was down from Sydney and we caught up later that day. She looked poised in a camel skivvy and black jeans, but I could see traces of exhaustion in her face. Over lunch she told me how important it was for Ben to get his rest and not overexert himself. 'We'll let you know when he's up to visitors,' she said. 'Olivia's staying in Melbourne for the next week. She can be our point of contact.'

I nodded, carefully absorbing the subtext of her words. At the end of lunch Charlotte said she was going to go back to the hospital for a short visit before she flew home to Sydney the next day. I understood why this was so, and why my situation was different, but felt subdued and fragile. It all felt very strange. Once again, there were no words to describe the emotions I was feeling. Something like the embarrassment of stumbling into rarefied heights where I didn't belong. The loss of something that never was.

My relationship with Ben and his children lacked the emotional dependency and shared closeness of upbringing that had created their social attachment. We hadn't been those things to each other and we would never have that bond. This hard kernel of truth was humbling. Unlike the others, I had been able to sleep the nights before and after his surgery. As Ben said quite plainly in *Australian Story*, 'Lauren's not my daughter socially. I had nothing to do with her life and she had nothing to do with my life, so she's not my daughter.' It had been a slow process to accept that our connection was something that doesn't have a name. And yet I am genetically as much his child as Charlotte, Michael, Olivia and my three unknown half-siblings. We all share the same chance of inheriting genetic advantages or flaws. Knowing about the family cluster of ependymomas might one day save my life, but this knowledge could just have easily remained buried.

That evening I felt confused. Confused about where I stood and what to do. I didn't want to do the wrong thing; I just didn't know what the right course of action was. On our walk the Sunday before, Ben had asked me to come and visit him in hospital on the Monday after his surgery. I didn't want to break that promise, but from what Charlotte had said the surgery had gone on longer than expected and his health was fragile. Visits were restricted to close relatives: partner and children only. I didn't want to go and see him just for my own benefit, only to score a point or satisfy my own ego, and potentially endanger his recovery. Probably the better thing was to spare him the effort and energy and let him rest. But on the other hand I worried that Ben would think I hadn't visited because I had forgotten, or couldn't be bothered, or didn't care. Maybe I should call the nurses and ask if he was up for a very brief visit. But how could I describe our label-less relationship on the phone? Would Charlotte be angry that I was circumventing her wishes? Perhaps the Clarks already felt I was being intrusive and were doing their best to tactfully ask me to retreat and give them some space. Maybe they were right; I was being intrusive.

On balance I decided the best course of action was to wait. Charlotte, Michael and Olivia could only spend a few days in Melbourne and soon had to return to their lives interstate. It was different for me; I lived in Melbourne, I was donor conceived, I could wait. Not naturally a very patient person, over years of searching I had learnt patience as my gait. 'The day will come,' donor-conceived people are constantly told. 'You just need to wait a little longer. Have patience for information, patience for understanding and patience for acceptance.' Rel was told to have patience for law reform that came too late.

Once again, the feeling crept back of occupying a strange, interstitial space, regressing from previous insights of unity glimpsed at the source of the Green River. It was true that at times I'd felt I could integrate all the branches of my family tree into one cohesive identity, but just as two wandering satellites can briefly align during an eclipse, this feeling waxed and waned. Ben's health crisis had brought back into focus the experience that has no name that I'd perceived on the day we first met. It is never quite finished, never quite resolved.

It's important to emphasise that this wasn't the fault of any individual; it wasn't about anything Ben or any other member of the Clark family had or hadn't said or done. As I mentioned earlier, the whole family has without exception been incredibly kind and welcoming and done their best to let me in as much as possible after I showed up unexpectedly. It wasn't my fault either, this vacuum. The incompleteness – the three half-siblings I know nothing about – was all institutionalised in the system that created me. We will never know exactly how many donor-conceived people were created in Australia (or indeed the world) because of the lack of accurate record keeping. Back when I was born it was a public system that was careless in the ways it fragmented biological and social bonds. Today it's a privatised system geared to profit, with a global reach.

Language controls the boundaries of how we can conceptualise and share our experiences with others. A person longing but unable to have a child has a word – *infertility* – to describe their experience. But the reverse condition does not have a name. Without specific words it's difficult to express this state to people who lack firsthand experience of it. But even before the word *gravity* was invented apples still fell to the earth.

Imagine trying to dance simultaneously to two pieces of music. Both express truth in their own way, but are discordant with each other. When overlaid, the rhythms can briefly synchronise, but inevitably pull away from one another. Likewise, there are parts of myself that are different from the family I grew up with that I catch glimpses of in the Clarks. But these people were all complete strangers until I was in my mid twenties and so I find myself orbiting like a satellite, always a little apart from their world, never quite knowing how I fit in. For a long time I searched for a way to bring these two melodies into harmony. I was drawn to the Sun Dagger, with its power to periodically unite the cycles of the sun and the moon, and the solar eclipse.

I was fortunate. Growing up, I'd had parents who each loved me in their own way, and in being so warmly welcomed by the Clarks I had the opportunity to discover many of my traits mirrored within this kinship group. Most people, including myself, thought that all I had to do was add these two experiences together to form a whole identity. But it wasn't as simple as that. I finally found clarity in accepting that both worlds are real and true in their own way, yet somehow they can't be mapped onto each other. There's a limitation; the two pieces don't quite fit, and from the core of their disjuncture is where the vacuum of incompleteness arises. Transition leaves lingering feelings of dissonance.

That night I had terrible dreams. I dreamt I went to visit Ben and his spine had been severed just below the neck. I touched his face and knocked him off balance. His severed head lay crooked, eyes closed, resting on the hospital pillow. I woke up feeling tired, foggy-headed and a little dizzy, like my subconscious was overwhelmed. I lay in bed scribbling notes, trying to jot down the essence of the dream before it faded. Gerry lay beside me for a while, then wordlessly got up and left the room. I joined him in the shower and could sense something was wrong.

'I'm sorry, I had some bad dreams.'

His silence warned me that I'd upset him.

'What's wrong?'

'I just feel excluded when you spend your whole day writing.'

I was being scripturient again. 'I'm sorry. I didn't mean to neglect you.'

As Charlotte had suggested, I contacted Olivia to ask her to keep me informed. This she did, and I really appreciated her consideration. I knew she was exhausted and strung out from the whole experience.

On Thursday morning I got confirmation from Olivia to come in for a visit. An hour later I got off the tram and crossed the road to the Royal Melbourne Hospital. When I walked into the room I saw Ben lying on the bed, quite formally dressed in a blue-checked shirt and camel trousers. Unusually, he was wearing shoes. He held a pillow over his head. Olivia stood up, gave me a warm hug and offered me the chair. Ben noticed someone was there and removed the pillow.

'Don't worry. I stick a pillow over my head all the time, and I haven't just had brain surgery,' I said, deadpan. 'So, how does it feel?'

'Bloody awful. Not because you just got here,' he reassured me.

I smiled.

'I've got a shocking headache, and vertigo, and feel as weak as a kitten.'

'That's not surprising, after what you've been through. You're not a Collingwood supporter now, are you?'

He gestured to a large white bag Olivia had brought in containing two yoga mats, a bottle of Shiraz and a black-and-white Collingwood beanie.

'Do you like yoga?' I asked Olivia.

'No, I hate it, but Andrew said it was the only thing that helped after his operation.'

'I looked up your surgeon,' I said to Ben. 'She looked great. She used to be a dentist.'

'Really? I should have had some dental work done while I was under.'

I laughed. 'Yeah, maybe a few fillings and a clean.'

Ben's sense of humour was intact. That was reassuring. A nurse came in to say he could be discharged soon, but she just had to finalise the paperwork. She asked if he wanted a wheelchair to get down to the transit lounge and Olivia said yes.

'Dad can walk,' she told me after the nurse left. 'He kept insisting on doing laps around the ward. I wore his slippers and they were so uncomfortable they gave me blisters so I was hobbling next to him.'

I laughed. 'It probably looked like you were the patient.'

Ben sat up. I noticed his shaved hair and the vertical bandage on the left side of his neck and head.

'Nice asymmetric haircut,' I quipped. 'Very hipster.'

'Thanks.' He cleared his throat. 'I asked the surgeon about the risk of a genetic link and the answer was still the same: they don't know.'

I was touched that at a time like this he had been so thoughtful as to follow up my question. I could see that he was putting in an effort because I'd come, and that it was costing him energy. Talking was most likely making his splitting headache worse. I understood why it had been necessary to minimise visits.

I started talking to Olivia to give Ben a break.

'How are you?'

'I'm better now. I've been so tired and muggy-headed, it sort of felt like I had brain surgery too.'

'You poor thing. You must be exhausted.'

Olivia told me about the acute care unit where they put Ben straight after the operation. Initially the nurses monitored him every five minutes and only one visitor was allowed in for literally sixty seconds at a time. There were twenty beds and some of the other patients weren't faring so well after their operations, with various degrees of neurological damage. A reminder of what might have happened. But in this universe, Ben had made it through; was standing up, doing laps of the ward, and despite his pain even making jokes. I was so relieved.

After Ben's partner, Sue, arrived to take him home, Olivia and I walked from the Royal Melbourne Hospital into the city. As we emerged into the warmth of the early spring sunshine I saw the strain on poor Olivia's face and realised that for the past week everyone had been hounding her for news and updates, myself included. She had really been doing her best.

As we walked and talked I told Liv about America.

'Are you planning on getting another job?' she asked.

'Eventually. I'm sort of ruined after taking time off from work to travel.'

'I know,' said Olivia. 'Sometimes I wish I hadn't spent a semester in Berlin so I didn't know how good it was.'

'Oh yeah, I'd love to hear more about that sometime. The art and music and history and everything must have been incredible.'

'Yeah, and the coffee.'

We parted ways at Elizabeth Street where we gave each other another warm hug.

'I'm coming back in November,' said Olivia. 'Hopefully under happier circumstances.'

'Let me know when you'll be in town.'

'You said you might be away?'

'I don't know where I'll be.'

'Don't worry. I don't know what I'm doing with my life either,' said Olivia.

I laughed. 'At least it's not just me.'

Twenty

After Ben's surgery Gerry terminated the lease on his shack and we spent two months camping through the Flinders and West MacDonnell ranges, contemplating our future.

Moving back to Australia had created a moment of choice. The easy decision was simply to return to our old Melbourne postcode, which seemed to offer the best mix of family, friends and economic prospects. But something made us pause. Over the past few years, living in the city had become harder. It was ever more expensive, and difficult to get around. Since my first nerve-wracking visit to meet Ben in Cape Paterson all those years ago, Gerry and I had developed an affinity with the rugged Bunurong coastline. The expansive ocean beckoned me to leave the city, but this intuition competed with the concern that I wouldn't be able to find a job.

The idea of the move continued to brew. A few weeks later we checked out a rental in the coastal town of Inverloch, just ten minutes past Cape Paterson. The simple wooden house was set on a large block in a leafy part of town. The living area looked out through a huge window on to a park with a picnic table and a scarred tree, a reminder this land is known by the stories of the Bunurong people. We loved the house and it was affordable, but when our application was accepted it created a dilemma. Like a repeat of my struggle to decide to leave work to travel in America, placing the deposit and first month's rent would make things real, while the idea of moving still felt like a pipedream.

We couldn't figure out what to do. After stalling for a few days, we took another trip to Inverloch and sat at the wooden picnic table in the park adjacent to the house.

'What do you think?' asked Gerry.

I paused, contemplating the reversed view looking back through the large window into the living room. 'It's lovely,' I admitted, and sighed. 'But how could we make it work? It just doesn't seem feasible.'

Reluctantly, I emailed the real estate agent and declined the offer.

Some family visited over the summer holidays and we spent a few nights camping in Cape Paterson. Mum and I took a trip to nearby Phillip Island and visited Saint Philip's Anglican Church in Cowes – a small, white, weatherboard church adorned with a simple wooden cross. Inside, hanging on the wall, was a brief history of the church. Behind framed glass, the timeline recounted that in 1921 Phillip Island became a parish in its own right. The vicar was listed as the Reverend CHC Clark – Manning's father, my great-grandfather.

The next day Gerry and I tried out a community yoga class in nearby Wonthaggi. After the class we happened to mention to the instructor that we had considered moving down to the Bass Coast. Her eyes widened in delight as she waxed lyrical about how much she enjoyed living there. Her enthusiastic description really sold the idea to us. As sometimes happens when a decision is so finely balanced, we let ourselves be persuaded by this random encounter with an unknown sage.

'Let's experiment,' suggested Gerry in the car. 'We can always move back to Melbourne if it doesn't work out.'

Something about the spaciousness of the ocean, in all her moods and glory, had caught my imagination.

'Okay,' I replied. 'Why not?'

Hearts racing, we called the real estate agent and found out the house was still available. We took it, and moved out of the city to live next to the sea, close to the water.

Gerry had already established a routine of working remotely so the main question was what I was going to do. Miraculously, days before moving in, I was approached on LinkedIn and signed a contract for a part-time job consulting remotely for another electric aircraft start-up, based in Sweden.

After moving into the Inverloch house at the end of January the stunning inlet and surf beaches invited us to take almost daily swims. When conditions were favourable – a northerly wind and low swell – we snuck away to indulge in a lunchtime snorkel and enjoy the incredibly rich and enchanting underwater world of the Bunurong Marine National Park. Like the desert, the far horizons of the ocean offered up space for my cluttered mind to expand into. Living on the coast and being surrounded by natural beauty crystallised my commitment to spend more time advocating for the environment. Through involvement with local groups we discovered a depth of community around Wonthaggi, a former company town for the State Coal Mine. The area retains something of a can-do, cooperative spirit.

Gerry and I started to put down roots and got to know a few people, who generously shared their special places with us newcomers. One morning I got a call and roused Gerry who jumped up from his desk. We raced to an ocean lookout near Phillip Island and our spontaneity was rewarded with views of two endangered southern right whales. They swam in close to shore and one vocalised a bellow, like an enormous sea cow, before flipping its tail out of the water as it dived beneath the waves.

Honouring our pledge, it became a ritual to walk down to the beach to appreciate the infinitely varied nature of each sunset: sometimes a pink mist, or a line of gold on the horizon. At certain times, just the right angle of sun and cloud would set the sky ablaze with a transcendent fire. I tried to name the sunset colours, but like my connection to the Clark family they resisted capture from the loose weave of the net of words.

Our bedroom in the house that almost slipped through our fingers faced east and Gerry and I made a pact to leave the curtains and windows open to better hear the rumble of the ocean, and let the chorus of birds and the dawn light wake us. There was something about this place that felt like home.

One weekend, listening to the clacking of wattlebirds drinking nectar from the banksias, I picked up a book from my bedside table. I'd first seen it two years earlier on Katerina's bookshelf in Connecticut. As I flipped through the pages I happened upon a passage that caught my eye.

'Historical consciousness is the unique and universal human compulsion to remember and make sense of the past … Humans are history makers. We record and remember our past. In other words, historical consciousness is part of the human condition.'

As I read the next sentence my heart started to pump a little faster.

'Being a link in a chain, not just a person in isolation, reveals a sense of gaining the immortality and timelessness of being part of a bigger story. Stories are the essence of how historical consciousness is transmitted from one generation to the next.'

The best books tell you what you already know. A flash of realisation lit up my brain. There *was* language to describe the ways our past, present and future are connected. It had a name: 'historical consciousness'. It was all part of an ancient story, happening everywhen. *A million shimmering ripples of cause and effect.* In turn, my mind brought to the surface the elusive question that I needed to ask myself: why was I searching for my roots?

That was it! To answer the question of what incited my search contained everything – the door to freedom in the centre of the mystery of my being finally revealed. Sometimes, as in this book, the answer comes before the question. The journey must follow a long, strange, self-referencing loop. *I am you and what you see is me.*

I closed my eyes and smiled, marvelling at the serendipity. I was no longer a tree without roots. My search for my family history had unearthed a family of historians. And now, looking forward, there was a new branch unfurling. Opening my eyes, I looked at the book I held in my hands. Titled, *Private Lives, Public History*, the author was none other than my cousin and doppelgänger, the historian Dr Anna Clark.

As an engineer and writer, over the years I've learnt that a willingness to look beyond the boundary of the verifiable can be rewarded with the beauty of truths unprovable. I gazed up from Anna's book through the open bedroom window at two magnificent eucalypts. Something about their rough, red, furrowed bark seemed familiar. But it wasn't until I remembered how an ecologist neighbour had described them as 'bastard mahoganies – out of range', that I realised what they were. The trees that can't survive without their roots entangled in the greater forest, their family. Bangalays.

Postscript

Gerry and I welcomed our daughter the following autumn. We named her after Australia's longest river, the Murray.

Acknowledgements

With deepest gratitude I acknowledge the following people for their contributions to the publication of this memoir that explores the little-known lived experience of being created from third-party reproduction:

The team at University of Queensland Press, in particular my publisher, Madonna Duffy, for her courage, clarity of vision and unwavering belief in me; Margot Lloyd, my amazingly talented editor who lovingly sharpened my words into points (sorry I still don't understand what a dangling modifier is!); and Sally Wilson, Kirsty Wilson and Louise Cornegé for their brilliant marketing and publicity.

My literary agent Jacinta di Mase, the boss of Australian publishing, for taking on a novice, and Anna Clark and Clare Wright for linking us.

TangledWebs, in particular Narelle Grech, Myf Cummerford, Pauline and Gordon Ley, Romana Rossi and Damian Adams, for their life-changing friendship and support.

The wonderful donor-conceived people who gave permission for me to share their words and stories, and our entire community and supporters, in which the smart, funny, talented and brave are uncommonly common; I hope I've done you justice and you can recognise elements of your own stories within mine.

Also acknowledging the generosity of Barbara Burns, Benedict Clark, Pauline Ley, Meredith Lemić, David de Kretser, Kate Dobby, Helen Kane, Kimberley Springfield, VARTA, MUP and the Victorian parliament for giving permission for their words to be reproduced in my book.

My family, in the broadest sense of the word, for their love, support and graciousness in allowing me to speak and write my mind, in particular my mother, Barbara Burns, for her help during the writing process.

Benedict Clark, for always saying 'yes' to me when 'no' might have seemed like the easiest answer.

Rowland Clark, for assisting in my two retreats at Ness that bookended the beginning and end of the writing process.

My early readers – my mother, Barbara; Gerry; my cousin Kathryn James; Ian Smith; Gaby Naher, who generously read my first draft; and Clare Wright, who provided invaluable feedback and encouragement at a critical juncture of the manuscript.

And finally: to Gerard Drew and our daughter, Murray Sunset, I hope you know all you mean to me. With you I'm home; like the birds, we squawk with the joy of flying through life together.